BEING
GLOBAL

BEING
GLOBAL

Making the Case for International Alumni Relations

GRETCHEN DOBSON

WASHINGTON, D.C.

The author wishes to thank the following people and institutions for permission to use these figures and art in this book: Ray Satterthwaite, Engagement Analysis, "Engagement Drivers," p. 23; the University of British Columbia, "UBC's Alumni Dashboard," p. 25; London School of Economics, "LSE Confidentiality Agreement," p. 46; Anderson School of Management, UCLA, "Anderson School of Management Travel Survey" (survey by SurveyMonkey), p. 91; INSEAD, "INSEAD Reunion Program Cover," p. 104.

Book design: O2 LAB
Art Director: Angela Carpenter Gildner
Editorial Director: Julie K. Schorfheide

COUNCIL FOR ADVANCEMENT
AND SUPPORT OF EDUCATION
1307 New York Avenue, NW
Suite 1000
Washington, DC 20005-4701
www.case.org

CASE EUROPE
3rd Floor, Paxton House
30 Artillery Lane
London E1 7LS
United Kingdom

CASE ASIA-PACIFIC
Unit 05-03
Shaw Foundation Alumni House
11 Kent Ridge Drive
Singapore 119244

In Memory of
Jenn

CONTENTS

The equation when considering international alumni relations is this:
> student + an educational experience outside the student's
> home country = an opportunity to build a lifetime relationship
> with a school, college or university

The equation is also this:
> graduating college senior or graduate student + the future =
> an opportunity to build a lifetime relationship with a college or university

And the equation may be this as well:
> a disengaged alum expat living abroad for the last 15 years +
> alma mater's international alumni relations strategy = opportunity

Finally, we have this equation:
> a growing number of undergraduate and graduate students
> studying at international institutions = reality

Being Global: Making the Case for International Alumni Relations was written to provide an assessment of how schools, colleges, universities and some business schools around the world are engaging with their international alumni. Until now, very little has been written on the subject, although it has been the topic of numerous conference sessions, breakfast roundtable discussions and webinars. (I've participated in these, and I would bet many of you have as well.) For years, the topic has been hardly more than a footnote to most advancement-related conferences.

For many institutions, international alumni relations is not a priority and will never be. Changes during the last decade, however, are causing more institutions to think again about their far-flung graduates: international student enrollments are on the rise, the cost of communicating with people outside one's own country is decreasing and individual mobility on a global scale is increasing.

This book, then, is for those institutions (independent schools, colleges and universities) that are wondering about how—or even whether—to undertake an international alumni relations program. It's also for those institutions that have decided to embark on such a program and would like to know more about how others are tackling the challenges and the key issues facing alumni professionals working internationally. And it's for everyone who is wondering what signifies a successful, exciting program with impact.

Is international alumni relations right for your institution? Let this book help you find the way to an answer.

ACKNOWLEDGMENTS

I wrote this book on a plane—many planes—and that is where I would like to start my appreciation.

I want to thank Tufts University for giving me the opportunity to build an advancement career, to travel throughout the world building relationships with our alumni and our regional chapters and to help instill a desire among international alumni to get involved and give back.

The people at Tufts University have provided the ongoing support to build our international alumni relations program. Acknowledgments begin with former Tufts University President Lawrence S. Bacow and former Senior Vice President and Provost Jamshed Bharucha. Their leadership and dedication to the university's international agenda provided a road map for much of my work. Vice President for University Advancement Brian K. Lee and Executive Director of Development Eric Johnson led our advancement team's strategic planning efforts for our current capital campaign. Both colleagues provided ongoing support, direction and opportunities throughout the last nine years as alumni relations prioritized our international plans. Many other colleagues on campus share in our international alumni relations story as well: Jo Wellins, Ming Zhong, Jennifer Simons, Jane Etish-Andrews, Michelle Hinkle and our colleagues from the Fletcher School of Law and Diplomacy.

Special thanks go to Tim Brooks, executive director of the Office of Alumni Relations. Tim has been my boss, my mentor and my advocate and served as a reader for this book. Tim's infectious enthusiasm for the work of alumni relations makes him a stand-out, and his close guidance and trust in my abilities gives me an opportunity to innovate, collaborate and, ultimately, produce results. To Brigid Burke, Ryan Earley, Sarah Keleher and my colleagues in the Office of Alumni Relations, thank you for sharing your enthusiasm for this book and for supporting me at all times.

This book was a product of collaboration with more than 60 alumni relations professionals from around the world, and I have included examples and best practices from most of these campuses. Many thanks to the following institutions and individual contributors for sharing your time, resources and programs:

Independent schools: the American School in Japan; Benenden School; Eton College; Hong Kong International School; International School Kuala Lumpur; 'Iolani School; Lincoln School; Phillips Exeter Academy; Singapore American School; Taipei American School; United World College of Southeast Asia; and the Woodstock School.

Colleges and universities: Australian National University; Bentley College; Central European University; Chinese University of Hong Kong; Cornell University; George Washington University; Imperial College; Indian Institute of Technology, Kanpur; London School of Economics; Massachusetts Institute of Technology; Michigan State University; National University of Singapore; Stanford University; University of Phoenix; Tufts University; University of British Columbia; University of Chicago; University de Navarra; University of Auckland, New Zealand; University of California at Davis; University of Cambridge; University of Michigan, Ann Arbor; University of Toronto; Yale University; and the State University of New York's Global Affairs Office.

Business school programs: Anderson School of Business at the University of California, Los Angeles; Haas School of Business at the University of California, Berkeley; Booth School of Business at the University of Chicago; IESE (Instituto de Estudios Superiores de la Empresa); INSEAD (Institut Européen d'Administration des Affaires–European Institute of Business Administration); Max M. Fisher College of Business at Ohio State University; Pepperdine School of Business; and Stanford Graduate School of Business.

A number of professional colleagues consulted on this book. I would like to acknowledge Andrew Shaindlin; Daniel Guhr; Ray Satterthwaite; Michael Stoner; and Elizabeth Scarborough.

I want to thank colleagues at CASE: Joanna Motion and Ben Prasadam-Halls for confirming that this was a worthwhile endeavor; and Rae Goldsmith, Krista Slade and John Lippincott for helping me identify so many of the institutions included in these pages. Julie Schorfheide, my editor at CASE, brought wisdom, organization and overall support to this project. I am extremely grateful to Julie for her expertise and guidance on what was an ambitious time line.

It's appropriate to thank my friends, many of whom are the Tufts alumni dotting the world and leading many of our programs. You know who you are, and I am honored to work closely with you and others every year. Keep up the great work.

Finally, to my family: You continue to be 3,000 miles away, but your love and support make you feel like you're right next door. I love you all.

INTRODUCTION

You've heard it many times: We're in the relationship business. Whether at independent schools, colleges, or universities, alumni relations professionals help forge and maintain ties between institutions and graduates. Those relationships begin, not at graduation, but when children, teenagers, and even adults first become students at an institution, and we strive to make them continue throughout each alum's lifetime.

These statements are true whether an institution's graduates live near or far—even if far now means on the other side of the globe.

Once students become graduates, institutions face many decisions about how to continue their relationships with their alumni. The decisions are made more complex as institutions are faced with the challenges presented by alumni overseas.

For institutions pondering whether to implement an international alumni program, or for those wishing to improve their existing program, this book can offer some guidance and insight.

In chapter 1, we'll look at how institutions decide whether to undertake an international alumni relations program. In assessing their readiness, institutions need to consider the following questions:

- Will the program support the institution's goals?
- What are the challenges of beginning and/or sustaining the program?
- What are the potential benefits?
- What resources will be required?

As with most undertakings in alumni relations, the answers vary from case to case. A school boasting a history of more than 100 years will have different considerations than more modern academies. Universities located in major metropolitan areas and business schools that provide international curricula and study-abroad experiences will answer these questions differently as well.

Chapter 2 looks at what constitutes a successful international alumni relations program. How do you define *success?* How do you measure it? What does a successful program look like?

Today, independent schools, colleges and universities are assessing their international alumni relations practices more than ever. The return on investment is a common evaluative marker, but applying it to alumni relations is difficult. Relationships take time and must be a priority for all, but geographic distances add challenges to these efforts. There are ways to measure the "healthiness" of this relationship, however, by using surveys, benchmarking and other tracking tools. Some institutions also find that linking international alumni relations and development can help make the case that their effort to engage students and alumni pays off.

Chapter 3 gives concrete illustrations of how various independent schools, colleges, universities and business schools around the world are running their programs and coping with many challenges. In this chapter, you'll see different ways to manage from a distance, learn ideas about student-alumni programming and programming with faculty, and look closely at a few signature programs.

The notion of "best practices" is one of the most important outcomes of the research behind this book. What one school does well in Asia may be exactly what a private school in the U.K. has wanted to try. A traditional event occurring every year for the last 75 years in the United States may make its debut in India in this decade. Read these sections on successes at other institutions and ask yourself whether there is something worth adapting to your campus. What makes one international relations program unique to its alumni can be the same feature that makes another program stand out for the first time.

Chapter 4 looks ahead to what might lie ahead for alumni relations—and what it means for professionals working in this field. It examines some common assumptions about alumni relations and whether they will remain valid through the next decade. How will international alumni relations professionals and our programs adapt to upcoming challenges and opportunities?

In the following chapters, you'll meet a variety of independent schools, universities and business schools from Australia, New Zealand, Canada, the United States, Europe and Asia. Read these pages as if you have assembled a peer group of international alumni relations professionals for your own focus group. What has been described above is a sample of questions and topics to explore. All together, their collective wisdom and enthusiasm for their work is something worth sharing.

CHAPTER 1

BUILDING THE CASE

Assessing Readiness for International Alumni Relations

Will the program support the institution's goals?

What are the challenges of beginning and/or sustaining the program?

What are the potential benefits?

When does an institution know it is "ready" to commit to international alumni relations?

For some, such as the University of Cambridge (founded in 1209), a uniquely long history may help in making this decision. Other schools, such as the London School of Economics, with a majority of international enrollees, or France's INSEAD, the "business school for the world," will find that their long-term commitment to pulling students from outside the institution's home country means that their alumni are indeed mostly international.

For most independent schools, colleges and universities and a majority of professional degree-granting institutions, however, the answer is not so obvious. Perhaps shifts in student demographics through the years have led to a substantial number of alumni who are far-flung rather than nearby. These institutions must make a deliberate decision whether to embrace "being global."

Sometimes, new leadership may prompt a shift in perspective, or comprehensive fundraising planning may be the impetus to push alumni relations and development teams to set up an international infrastructure. Or it may be the case that these factors simultaneously create an opportunity to become deliberately active overseas.

The decision to embark on an international alumni relations program should take into account a number of factors:

Will it support your institution's goals?

What are the challenges of beginning and/or sustaining the program?

What are the potential benefits?

SUPPORTING YOUR INSTITUTION'S GOALS

It almost goes without saying that you should consider your institution's objectives before deciding to undertake an international alumni relations program. Doing so will help you say "no" if it's becoming clear that such a program isn't right for your school (no matter how much certain groups want it to happen) or will help you persevere in the face of obstacles you will encounter. Keeping the institution's goals in mind will also help focus the goal of the international program itself.

The Tufts Experience

At Tufts University in the greater Boston metropolitan area, our international alumni relations program developed in conjunction with other university stakeholders. The International Board of Overseers (IBO) has been a major player in this effort.

The IBO provides guidance to the administration on issues related to the international aspects of education at Tufts; links to the international research, political and philanthropic communities that are essential constituencies of the university; and philanthropic leadership and stewardship for the programs and educational experiences that make Tufts one of the most international of U.S. universities. Its goals include improving and expanding the international reputation and reach of Tufts' students, alumni, parents, faculty and friends and ensuring that the Tufts experience is as international as possible in this increasingly interdependent world. (See sidebar "More About the IBO.")

The arrival of a new president in 2001 and a new provost in 2002 coincided with the beginning of a capital campaign in 2002. Tufts' global outlook became one of the central themes of the campaign, and the IBO worked closely with university leadership to develop a three-country, five-year plan by which Tufts would target countries identified as future strategic partners. IBO members, key regional hosts committees, the Fletcher School of Law and Diplomacy and administration and faculty coordinated trips to Mexico (2004), India (2005) and China (2007). These countries were chosen both for their rising positions in the global community and for the number of alumni and applicants living in them. Tufts wanted to build relationships with the alumni and parent bases in each country, increase student recruitment opportunities and promote research collaboration and student exchange programs.

What started in the 1980s and 1990s as a group of internationally connected alumni and parents interested in meeting as a board and hobnobbing over wine and cheese in cities such as Paris and London has now become a purposeful and committed advisory group.

Established by Tufts University's Board of Trustees, the International Board of Overseers serves as a vitally important resource to the president and to the trustees as they work to guide the further development of Tufts' excellence and contributions nationally and internationally.

Through the years, the composition of Tufts' IBO has changed. "It's becoming more international. Attention has been paid to adding members from the regions that have been visited," according to Michelle Hinkle, director of the Board of Overseers Office. "We're sensitive to diversity in age, culture and gender. We have friends, alumni, parents and even university trustees involved. Our current board chair is a parent from Switzerland."

The IBO has approximately 30 active members, representing 10 countries. Board members serve for five-year terms; terms may be renewed once. Continuity in board leadership helps orientate newcomers and provides advocacy in initiatives such as adding more international events and alumni chapters. The board meets twice a year. Spring meetings take place at Tufts' European campus in Talloires, France. Fall meetings have been held during the Tufts in the World trips.

Since its trip to China in 2007, the IBO has refocused on its role as an advocate for the university. "We're actively engaging our board members as meeting hosts and speakers at regional alumni events. This [ambassador] role is something they requested, and I will work with the advancement staff in creating more opportunities," says Hinkle.

Tufts is always on the lookout for potential IBO members for future years. Board members may be nominated at any time. Nominations are reviewed and voted upon by the Board of Trustees' Executive Committee. Official invitations are formally extended by the president.

Each trip of the "university road show"—formally known as Tufts in the World—was held in the fall and included admissions presentations to secondary school counselors and students as well as evening receptions open to the entire Tufts community: alumni, parents, friends, corporate partners and other designated guests. Influential alumni and parents from these regions sponsored receptions, which were held in distinctive locations such as museums, cultural centers and government function halls. Each special event and individual meeting offered opportunities to develop interest in starting alumni chapters in Mexico, India and China.

As Tufts' international alumni relations program grows, it supports the larger goals of the university as a whole.

Increasing Engagement

Perhaps your institution's goal is to increase engagement with your overseas alumni to encourage volunteerism, enhance recruitment, or support fundraising efforts. Some schools leverage their curriculum to expose students, faculty and international alumni to each other. Business schools provide good examples. (See chapter 3 for more examples.)

For the last 18 years, Ohio State University's Max M. Fisher College of Business has offered the Emerging Markets Field Study, in which students focus on the history, politics, culture and business environment of an emerging market economy. During each 10-week course, students also design a business project for the country. Alumni are invited to attend the course, be on a project team or take part in a field study. One or two alumni usually participate in the field-study aspect of the course.

The University of Toronto has increased its engagement with overseas alumni by opening a satellite office in Hong Kong. "We have an international alumni relations staff based in Toronto," says Jeremy Woodall, formerly at U of T's advancement office in Hong Kong, now director of the University of Oxford's China office. "Because we are here in Hong Kong, we know so many more alumni and are involved more directly in their lives. This strongly encourages alumni volunteerism. They help us staff events around the region."

Bentley University in Waltham, Mass., set up a satellite office in Madrid in 2006, which was run by Jennifer Aquino until her departure in July 2009. Bentley's institutional goal was to develop the area of international fundraising, and Aquino knew she would meet the university's goals more quickly if she also focused on building stronger international alumni relations.

Bentley does not have a formal chapter program for its overseas alumni, but groups of alumni have formed in London, Geneva, Athens, Mumbai, Delhi, China, Taiwan, Hong Kong, Bangkok and Panama. To keep in touch with the alumni and to track engagement, Aquino sent out a quarterly international alumni report. She gathered news from admissions and other departments with academic ties to programs abroad. Alumni would write back inquiring about how to start an alumni group.

Bentley also set up an International Alumni Council (IAC). Like the IBO at Tufts, IAC advises Bentley on its international strategies. Alumni involved with the IAC provided an important service to Bentley by thinking of ways the college's brand could be enhanced.

During her tenure, Aquino looked at internal measures of engagement such as satisfaction rates and, for those who immediately participated, a willingness to get involved at another time. "The alumni are evaluated by how they feel they can connect to each other and how they feel about Bentley being on the map," says Aquino.

FIG. 1.1　|　THE FOUR PILLARS OF ENGAGEMENT

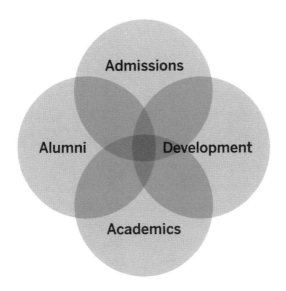

Other Goals

Does your institution want to strengthen its presence outside its home country? Does it hope to diversify its student base or even open a campus in another country? Perhaps the main goal is to encourage more giving from alumni overseas.

These goals are often intertwined, as figure 1.1 illustrates. How do the "four pillars of engagement" fit into your institution's goals and strategy? Is the strategy to develop and support admissions efforts, alumni communities, academic programs and partnerships, all in an effort to build a strong case for support? Can the "three A's"—admissions, alumni and academics—provide enough evidence to institutional leadership, prospective students and prospective donors that they should support a strengthened presence in a particular region of the world?

CHALLENGES

What are the key issues facing alumni professionals working internationally?

Culture

U.S.-based institutions that are assessing their chances of success in attracting international attention, participation and support from their alumni in a variety of countries would be making a mistake to think that alumni are the same all over the world. The idea of building a community for your institution around a common cause or concern can be a uniquely different undertaking in each country. We can all think of examples of a cultural faux pas, and many books cover the topic of cultural differences quite well.

Organizational models will also vary according to culture. Figure 1.2 shows some basic differences between a chapter in Asia and one in the United States, for example. Emphasis placed on hierarchy and "rank" are commonplace in Asia, as in the notion that a more senior member of the leadership is the figurehead and spokesperson while more junior (whether in age or professional experience) members are valued "do-ers" who are on the ground locally to assist the university. In the United States, organizational structures are flatter, more communal, and more casual: group efforts are more commonplace, meaning that several alumni contribute equally to outreach, programming and representation.

Be sensitive and adaptable to cultural norms and expectations when arranging logistics for events. In the United States, you might publicize an event about three weeks in advance, but in Switzerland, for example, you should start the publicity at least two to three months ahead of the date. In India or Mexico, on the other hand, a week or slightly more is fine. In my experience working in India and Mexico, I have become comfortable knowing that I don't know the exact nature of the guest lists a few days before events. I expect a last-minute surge of interest in the event and leave plenty of time before and after the actual event time line for last-minute preparations. Conversations at these events will often linger on well after the "official" event close, and very often, I will find myself invited to meet

> **TIP**
>
> During my work for Tufts, I have found that Parisians are eager to socialize and educate themselves (when a road show with university faculty arrives); but because their government provides many basic services, French alumni are less prone to spend time volunteering with disadvantaged populations. In India, more participants will come from prospective families seeking information and contacts from the U.S. school. The chance of "getting a leg up" with a personal contact is a highly valuable commodity for a middle- to upper-class Indian family.

FIG. 1.2 | ORGANIZATIONAL MODELS ACROSS CULTURES

ALUMNI CHAPTERS IN ASIA	ALUMNI CHAPTERS IN THE U.S
» Formal model	» Formal and informal models
» Older, more senior alumnus is honorary leader	» Steering committees lead by co-chairs distribute responsibilities
» Junior members carry out functional duties of chapter	» Chapters usually identify at least one person as contact to central office
» Deference paid to leader	» Succession planning key
» Best model occurs when there is good communication between all officers and central alumni relations office	» Many are lead by younger alumni and types of events may reflect generational interests
» In-person relations is key	» Chapter events may be planned more spontaneously
» Advance planning respected	
» Chapter events should include family	

alumni and/or parents for coffee, a drink or a meal at another time during the trip. Leave room in your schedule for impromptu appointments. These can be the most enjoyable part of a trip, as you learn more about a culture from personally experiencing a home-cooked meal or an alumnus's workplace environment.

You will encounter cultural differences, but your alumni will be eager to help you navigate the unfamiliar terrain, and a willingness on your part to learn and adapt will help establish good relations all around.

If your institution is outside the United States and is interested in developing alumni relations programs in that country, you might want to form a multigenerational steering committee for the program. Recruit some younger alumni, others of middle age (15 to 20 years out) and who are more seasoned (25+ years from graduation). Consider asking a prominent alumnus to be a "founding member" of the chapter, as his or her name will provide enough cachet and legitimacy to attract followers. This committee can advise the planning process and facilitate alumni relations. In the United States, alumni events are commonplace, and having a breadth of volunteers will better assure success with outreach and program types.

Staffing, Budget and Other Resource Issues

Make no mistake: Starting and sustaining an international alumni relations program is a costly undertaking. Staff interested in working internationally will soon assess their opportunities of success by looking both at the budget allotted to international alumni relations and at how these resources support the development of programs that resonate with alumni overseas. Consider these questions surrounding resources:

- Will you need more staff? Will staff travel for in-person contact, or will you handle your outreach through social media and/or more traditional communication channels?
- Which geographic areas make the most strategic sense for growing an international program? (Remember the importance of supporting your institution's goals!)
- Should you open a satellite office to support your efforts? (See discussion below, under "Opportunities.")
- Are there internal stakeholders who might also benefit from international outreach? (See figure 1.3.) What are their international goals? Are they open to working across departments, disciplines and deans?
- You'll need to reassess resource allocation as your program grows or changes in other ways. Economic events can affect resources as well. Fiscal challenges are nothing to be secretive about: let the alumni know that resources are strained and ask them to help you think creatively about ways to promote the institution and regional relationships. (Chapter 2 addresses new ways of thinking about the international alumni relations budget.)

Volunteer Management

Having a dedicated, enthusiastic cadre of alumni volunteers in countries around the world can be a valuable resource for your institution and international alumni relations efforts, but establishing and maintaining such groups can be a huge task. Offer training sessions,[1] and define boundaries with a risk management strategy and written guidelines. Be clear about what the volunteers can and cannot do when acting in a capacity related to your institution. Being sensitive to cultural contexts will help you manage your volunteers well. Recognizing that volunteers lead busy personal and professional lives, establish a routine for communicating (e.g., monthly conference calls) and always be mindful of their own travel and holiday schedules, which may be different from your home institution's.

You'll need to maintain the volunteers' enthusiasm as well. Will visits from the "home team" suffice to keep ties strong, or will you need to make additional efforts? Annual visits will definitely help build community. I like combining a visit with an annual business meeting, a new volunteer recruitment night and plenty

FIG. 1.3 | POTENTIAL STAKEHOLDERS

INTERNAL PARTNERSHIPS	EXTERNAL PARTNERSHIPS
» Faculty, current and emeriti	» Parents – current and former
» Deans and chancellor or president	» Consulates, chambers of commerce, government agencies
» International students and scholars, full-time or part-time in special programs	» Internationally placed schools and campus units
» Alumni and development staff	» Foundations and other external sources of financing
» Student affairs units that influence recruitment and retention of international students and scholars	» Media—Education editors
	» Satellite office staff
» Communications	» Consortia
	» Professional associations
» Support units for research, data management	» Corporations

of social time to get to know my colleagues on a personal level and vice versa. It will be impossible to be everywhere, however, and I will try to send an event box in advance of a program with inexpensive giveaway items, copies of our *Tufts Magazine*, and a banner if requested. An encouraging email in advance of a gathering is always appreciated.

The Tufts Experience, Part 2

When I started at Tufts in 2002, the university had alumni chapters in London, Greece and Hong Kong. Tufts worked with these groups to host a reception every few years (or more often) for the university president and other high-level officials. Their focus was purely fundraising, not grassroots alumni relations work.

That began to change in 2003. Tufts' new president, who had been named in 2001, was being introduced to U.S. alumni and supporters through a city-based tour. I suggested that this concept be extended overseas. President Bacow traveled to London in December 2003, and we continued the "tour" in Paris and Switzerland in 2004, working strategically with the admissions office to sponsor an accepted-students reception for alumni, parents and friends as well as for the prospective students and families accepted as of April 1. For Tufts, the month of April has become an annual time for the admissions office and the alumni relations office to partner around the world, and these annual receptions have strived to feature high-level Tufts leaders. Thinking strategically about the timing of our trips and the relationships we made (we met many prospective students and families) the university's IBO fall trips to Mexico City, India and China were followed up with admitted student receptions the following April. It was another opportunity to invite participation and interest in Tufts.

The goal of these receptions was to jump-start our international alumni relations program with selected city events, high-level speakers and an ongoing, consistent staff member (me) at the forefront of the action.

Our budgets also increased to support this work. It was evident after the first year of international programs and from the increased interest from overseas alumni that we should invest extra money into this new series of programs. For example, an alumni and faculty authors series toured the United States and international chapters.

> **TIP**
>
> Whether you are working in the United States or overseas, personal contact is essential to success. You must spend time (on the phone or in person) with the potential alumni chapter representatives and ask them direct questions about why they are interested in getting involved. Knowing their goals at the onset will guide the future outreach efforts, programs and the university's expectations for working in another country.

The economic downturn of 2008 affected our budget, staffing and international programming. Hiring was frozen, and our professional international and domestic alumni relations team consisted of two people: my regional programs officer and me. An open FTE was not filled for another year.

Working within a strained environment (fewer staff, less money) was a valuable experience that continues to affect how we make decisions. During the 2008–2009 academic year, we looked at the demographics of our student body and our alumni and at our ability to sponsor programs in the United States and abroad with the financial support of others and asked: Was a program "necessary" or was it just "nice"? Knowing we had a growing number of students attending Tufts from Turkey and South Korea, we moved forward on programs in those countries and thought twice about extending our reach into Brazil or Puerto Rico that year.

Even with fiscal resources continuing to be tight, Tufts' international alumni relations program has been able to maintain consistent and adequate investments in people and programs. We now have 27 international chapters, and I don't think it will be easy to grow further. Our relationships with alumni, parents and internal and external partners are sustaining our work during these challenging years.

OPPORTUNITIES

Despite some ongoing challenges, the world is open to building relationships and, for some institutions, economic and demographic shifts are the impetus for branching out to their alumni.

International Alumni Relations and International Giving

Partly as a result of the global economic crisis of 2008, more institutions are paying attention to their international alumni, parents and other funding streams abroad. Additionally, the international arena is a logical place in which alumni relations and development offices can cooperate and collaborate to the benefit of both. "An international effort expands a college's pool of potential donors; helps keep the college in touch with alumni in other countries who may also be able to help in other ways, including admissions; and helps stimulate interest among international students," according to the *Chronicle of Higher Education*.[2]

It's important to maintain a relationship with alumni for many reasons, no matter where they live. But which is more important: the relationship as an alumni relations function or as a development function?

"You can't raise money without strong connections with your constituents, so time and effort will need to be put into cultivating events, organizing alumni chapters, and involving volunteers," according to Jeffrey A. Schoenherr, Harvard Law School's executive director of development and alumni relations. "It is especially important to people in some cultures to have a strong relationship before they talk of philanthropy."[3]

What motivates international alumni and parents to donate? Perhaps donors want to support scholarship opportunities for students applying from their home region to an international school, or they want to raise money locally to build a satellite office. Alumni and parents also may feel a strong urge to help a local cause. Alumni reunions could bridge the interest of alumni and the need of the charity *and* alma mater.

Picture a new regional reunion program for the alumni who cannot return to campus to celebrate their milestones. Plenty of annual giving appeals have occurred before the start of reunions. Now, part of the regional celebrations include some component that speaks to a local need and to how the alumni are helping benefit their community. Perhaps members of the reunion class in the institution's home country challenge their international alumni classmates to pledge certain hours of service; in return, these members match the hours of service with a set amount of money to their class fund. There is a lot of room for creativity!

The question we should be asking is whether a developed international alumni relations program is going to assist in the overall international fundraising agenda. It cannot hurt to have a network of strategically placed local volunteers to serve as facilitators. There is nothing to hide in today's economic reality. Be transparent and ask for help.

Overseas Study Still on the Rise

Another compelling reason to look outside your institution's home country is the increasingly international nature of student bodies. In 2009–2010, the number of international students at U.S. higher education institutions was at an all-time high. Students from China rose 30 percent, making up 18 percent of all international higher education students in the United States; students from India increased by 2 percent and accounted for 15 percent of international students in the United States.[4]

Canadian universities have also reported record international enrollments, thanks to more aggressive recruitment strategies, relationship-building efforts abroad and streamlined application processes.[5]

Institutions outside North America are seeing an influx of students from overseas as well. With limited opportunities to find jobs at home, recent graduates (from 2009 and 2010) are looking to relocate, to temporarily volunteer, and to consider graduate school programs overseas. More European business schools are attracting students from the United States and other countries, primarily Asia.[6]

The growing number of students from Korea, China and India who are now educated in the United States, Australia, Canada and the United Kingdom return home with professional degrees in hand to accept management positions with multinational firms. Their salaries in these countries support a better quality of life while they are advancing their careers. It is no wonder that so many institutions are now focusing on international alumni relations in Asia and India.

Satellite Offices

Brand Extension

Although we talked about satellite offices under the "challenges" section above, they can also be viewed as opportunities. One of the most visible ways to increase international branding is to hang your institution's sign in another country by opening a satellite office. This does not happen overnight. Successful satellite offices result from considering four primary factors: cost, scale, programmatic priorities and opportunity.[7] With each consideration, international alumni figure prominently in the decision to set up shop overseas.

Setting up a satellite office can be compared to dating someone at a distance. There will be multiple visits; over time, a growing amount of effort and money is invested in the relationship. Finally, one of the pair decides to move closer to reap the benefits of mutual support, sharing the same community and having a stronger chance to sustain the relationship over time. There are cost savings as well, but this is not the main benefit, since money saved by less travel to the region will be used to operate the "new home" or satellite office.[8]

Advancement offices are deciding it is time to capitalize on the relationships of not one, but many. A substantial percentage of alumni in a particular area provide the scale and, in turn, more opportunities for alumni engagement as volunteers, ambassadors and advocates for their alma mater. An informed and involved alumni base will be one of the most important criteria for satellite office success. Satellite offices with devoted regional staff and programs may aid in the development of stronger alumni relations; conversely, an engaged and active international community may be the exact partner desired by regional staff to ensure their success when opening an overseas office.

> ## TIP
>
> It's important to equip international volunteers with current and easy-to-explain mechanisms for giving. Whether they will be making local phone call appeals or referring a fellow alumnus to a tax-efficient vehicle for giving, the level of customization of each giving vehicle cannot be underestimated.
>
> From Luna Sidhu, "Internationalizing the Annual Fund," in *Across Frontiers,* ed. John Mc Loughlin and Jane Joo Park (Washington, DC: CASE, 2010), 61–72.

Regional Outreach

The University of British Columbia's Asia-Pacific regional office has been open in Hong Kong for more than 10 years. Made possible by a donation from an alumnus, the office has grown from a single-staff office to support the Hong Kong chapter to a multipurpose administrative arm for UBC in the region. Five staff members oversee student recruitment, study-abroad programs, academic exchanges and research support, in addition to alumni relations and development functions.

The newest office opened in the last few years in China. One of the inaugural programs held at the China office was Research Week, a multiday showcase of outstanding research led by UBC faculty and deans.

For the next Research Week program, in December 2009, faculty and deans traveled to major cities in Asia and presented day-long seminars organized according to discipline. The programs facilitated many introductions to key academics and prominent alumni. Alumni received an "insider's view of hot topics" and were able to give input on which topics would be on the program.

It is not always easy to match the right academic topic, faculty talent, and schedules. UBC faced these challenges in 2010 and decided to take a different approach by highlighting local research partnerships and how UBC's work influences the local economy. The university president's visits across Asia focused on these themes. Alumni involved in the program are well-versed about the objectives of the president's trip and helped promote the events locally.

UBC also used its China office as a venue for its regional volunteer summit. UBC subsidized a portion of travel costs for alumni leaders from across Asia. Staff members believe their investment in the program creates an opportunity for UBC to leverage the enthusiasm of a growing group of alumni volunteers to help the university create a strong presence in China.

Harvard Law School's Schoenherr emphasizes the importance of building an institution's brand internationally, since "many institutions are known abroad for something specific. Whether medicine, science, or the arts, every college and university has a brand that alumni, parents, prospective students, and even donors like to tout." [9]

Ohio State University (OSU) has taken steps to internationalize its institution. By building an office in China, OSU hopes to provide academic exchange and orientation for faculty and students, admissions contacts and services, alumni engagement, event space and a hub for executive education. [10] OSU's presence in Asia is a clear sign that the region is an institutional priority and affords an opportunity to align OSU's strengths with those of international partners.

Satellite Office Profile: Bentley University in Madrid

As mentioned earlier, Bentley University has had a satellite office in Madrid since 2006. About 5,000 alumni from Bentley's undergraduate and graduate programs live outside the United States.

It took three years from the time Bentley's vice president of corporate alumni relations and development made his first pitch to the Board of Trustees for a satellite office to the time of hiring Jennifer Aquino to manage the university's international work from Madrid.

Aquino sent out a quarterly report to international alumni to increase engagement, but she didn't "do events." Rather, she worked strategically with faculty and the deans on a more ad hoc basis. After traveling to the Persian Gulf with Bentley's president in 2008, she accompanied a faculty member to the same location in 2009 so he could pitch an idea to build an Islamic banking course in the Middle East, to be offered during January break.

The two met with alumni contacts and their colleagues in the banking sector and asked for their involvement in the start-up course. Some alumni contributed to the program, some were willing to host the program and some even offered to finance it.

Working one-on-one with individual faculty on their goals for their work in the region created a unique opportunity for an advancement officer to remain on the forefront of information. Aquino's quarterly report to alumni was peppered with examples of the most current academic information coming out of the regional office. Sharing the outcomes of recent meetings with alumni was both educational and personal.

Consortia: The Power of Many

Partnering with other institutions can be a tremendous way to increase impact. At Tufts, we've learned to welcome programming partners when planning large-scale international events; to participate in annual conversations about international alumni relations with institutions in our local (U.S.) area; and to ask international alumni with graduate degrees from international institutions for introductions to their alumni relations staff.

Large-Scale Events

In early 2004, the Tufts Alumni London leaders discussed sponsoring a panel on the impact of the U.S. presidential elections abroad. As the race heated up between incumbent President George W. Bush and Massachusetts Sen. John Kerry, the alumni thought this could be a well-attended program if scheduled in London a few weeks before Election Day. Alumni leaders serving on the panel at the program included graduates from Tufts' Fletcher School of Law and Diplomacy. They made a collective decision to bring the university alumni chapter together with the Fletcher School London Club to sponsor the program. Then they took another step. With an international topic in one of the world's most international cities, they invited the other major U.S. foreign-service preparation programs (Columbia, Johns Hopkins and Georgetown Universities) to join other universities and their alumni groups as co-sponsors. Each school agreed to take on a piece of the planning, including additional speaker recruitment, and each advertised the event to their London-based constituents. This was a critical step in attracting more than 300 guests.

The success of the four-university panel in 2004 has led to an annual program covering an international topic, such as "The Politics of Energy." The partnership creates opportunities for each alumni group to showcase a faculty or alumni speaker, builds rapport among the universities and maximizes attendance while minimizing out-of-pocket costs.

Annual Conversations

When international alumni relations officers are NOT traveling, consider inviting a range of institutions in your home region to a meeting about international alumni relations. In Boston, this get-together is called the International Alumni Relations Roundtable. Campuses take turns hosting the meeting, which is usually held in the late fall or early winter and again in the late spring or early summer. The Boston consortium has been meeting since 2008.

In preparation for the meeting, the host institution asks participants to provide an update on their international alumni statistics, activities and any new topics they want to discuss. (Schools unable to attend are encouraged to provide a sketch of their international activities.) This information generates a composite report of the participants' collective outreach; reports of individual efforts are made available as well. The information is also used as the basis for planning small group discussions or activities. For these activities, institutions are generally grouped by level of experience in international alumni relations (established programs versus schools just starting their outreach), but often a more experienced international alumni relations officer is assigned to the "start-up" group.

Host institutions should invite their senior advancement officer to welcome the group. Invitations may also be extended to admissions officers who recruit internationally, international program directors, international development officers and other members of your campus teams who are stakeholders in international programs.

> **TIP**
>
> Jeremy Woodall, director of the University of Oxford's China office, agrees for additional reasons: "Connect with alumni affairs professionals at local universities to find out what the expectations are for that region."

Introductions to Other Alumni Relations Staff

Finally, plan time in the travel schedule to network with other advancement staff. The Tufts Alumni London leader is also a graduate of the London Business School (LBS). In December 2005, she suggested that I meet with the director of alumni relations for LBS. I welcomed the introduction and, on my next trip to London, in January 2006, found myself having tea at her office. It was from that meeting that I learned about LBS World Day, a one-day celebration for alumni in London and other locations. Tufts had several new domestic and international alumni chapters, and I quickly envisioned a World Day program working well for the university. The public phase of our $1.2 billion comprehensive campaign would be launched in November 2006, and a World Day event in October would be another way to mobilize alumni support for Tufts and its regional chapters just weeks before the announcement. In the end, it was a great success. I encourage everyone to survey their alumni to determine whether your current programs could benefit from this type of expanded networking.

Independent Schools Working Together

Advancement professionals at independent schools have also realized the benefits of networking and sharing ideas. The Interscholastic Association of Southeast Asian Schools (IASAS) provides a model of successful collaboration.

IASAS was founded in 1982 as an athletics association, but its members now partner in other ways as well. In February 2008, the six schools that are now a part of IASAS—International School Bangkok, International School of Kuala Lumpur, International School Manila, Jakarta International School, Singapore American School and Taipei American School—held an alumni reunion in New York City. Headmasters from each of the schools traveled to the New York area to recruit students, and one night was reserved for schools to come together for an IASAS information session. School administrators from admissions, development and alumni relations were also available, and alumni based in New York City were present to answer questions from prospective students (as well as to enjoy their own networking opportunity). Alumni were encouraged to wear their school colors and/or logos. With planning and promotions handled by email, the event was a cost-effective way of promoting the schools in the United States.

CONCLUSION

The investment required to fulfill a comprehensive international plan is significant. Careful coordination with independent alumni associations, academic departments, professional schools, student services and other university stakeholders, such as admissions offices and the university's governing boards, is essential.

If we want more international alumni to participate in the future well-being of the institution, should we be thinking about sustainable ways to keep them engaged?

Do we eliminate models of organization, such as chapters and groups, and consider communication models as our sole avenue for engaging our international alumni?

How will we deploy staff to work most efficiently with an increasing number of alumni from a diversity of countries, states and regions? Will advancement professionals be located overseas full-time?

What types of formal training will be most beneficial to international alumni volunteers?

As we assess our most active international hubs, how ready are we for an international alumni relations effort, as gauged by the four pillars of engagement (figure 1.1)?

Having analyzed your ability to support your institution's goals, as well as the challenges and opportunities of international alumni relations work, do you feel that you have a better understanding of why you are (or could) commit to international alumni relations? Can you provide a few solid reasons for spending money, time and resources on these activities and would these be the same reasons others at your institution might offer?

The next step is to track your progress. Measuring the case for international alumni relations provides an opportunity to assess your "current standard operating procedures."

ENDNOTES

1. See Gretchen Dobson, "Programming Internationally," in *Alumni Relations: A Newcomer's Guide to Success*, 2nd ed., ed. John A. Feudo (Washington, DC: CASE, 2009), 257–67.

2. Kathryn Masterson and Chris Thompson, "Colleges Increasingly Look Abroad to Raise Funds," *Chronicle of Higher Education*, Feb. 3, 2010, *chronicle.com/article/Colleges-Increasingly-Look/63878/*.

3. Jeffrey A. Schoenherr, "International Fund Raising: It's Not Just About the Money," *Chronicle of Higher Education*, March 14, 2011, *chronicle.com/article/International-Fund-Raising-/126708/*.

4. Institute of International Education, Open Doors 2010, *www.iie.org/en/Who-We-Are/News-and-Events/Press-Center/Press-Releases/2010/2010-11-15-Open-Doors-International-Students-In-The-US*.

5. Aisha Labi, "Top Destinations Compete for Growing Numbers of Foreign Students," *Chronicle of Higher Education*, Nov. 16, 2009.

6. Katherine Mangan, "Global Focus Draws Students to Europe for Business," *Chronicle of Higher Education*, Sept. 26, 2010.

7. Donald Kirkwood, "Satellite Offices," in *Across Frontiers: New International Perspectives on Educational Fundraising*, ed. John Mc Loughlin and Jane Joo Park (Washington, DC: CASE, 2010), 73–85.

8. Ibid.

9. Schoenherr, "International Fund Raising: It's Not Just About the Money."

10. Karin Fischer, "Colleges Set Up Their Own Embassies Abroad," *Chronicle of Higher Education*, April 25, 2010.

CHAPTER 2

MEASURING THE CASE
How Do You Define Success?

What does "success" look like?

What is benchmarking?

What is meant by "engagement"?

How do institutions evaluate and maintain their programs?

_____

In this chapter, we'll take a look at how schools, universities and business schools are evaluating their current programs and determining what constitutes success in those efforts. How do we measure—and maintain—success?

In identifying what works best, you will need to evaluate current practices, develop goals and measurement tools and be honest about your resources. Think long-term with other key decision-makers, including your alumni abroad.

Before we move forward to learn about ways to engage with our international alumni, let's think about ways to define and measure success.

BENCHMARKING SUCCESS

The International CASE Alumni Relations Survey (ICARS), launched in 2005, is building "a statistical picture of what success looks like."[1] Participation in ICARS is open only to institutions outside North America, but any CASE member institution can read the analysis of each year's survey to learn "which alumni services and activities are statistically associated with greater success, and what successful AR programs do *more* of than less successful programs."[2]

ICARS participants have agreed that a "successful AR program" would be one whose numbers of attendees, volunteers and donors were in the top one-third of results reported by the 85 participants of the 2010 survey. To be in the top third (that is, to be "successful," according to ICARS' definition of success), you would need to have had at least 158 attendees, 23 volunteers and 139 donors per 10,000 constituents.[3]

ICARS is just one example of how alumni relations professionals have started assessing their programs more critically and measuring their efforts against those of other institutions—how they have started to benchmark their programs, in other words. Benchmarking is also possible for alumni relations programs that don't qualify to participate in ICARS, of course. For example, the CASE Benchmarking Toolkit, available to CASE member institutions, allows "peer communities of practice to design and conduct their own surveys, review results, and instantly download charts directly into reports."[4] Your institution can also find consultancies that will conduct benchmarking surveys.

Benchmarking isn't new to alumni relations. In 1985, CASE published *Criteria for Evaluating Advancement Programs*, a book about program self-assessment. Over the years, two types of benchmarking in alumni relations have developed. Operational benchmarking "looks at inputs and outputs: how many alumni you have; the size of your budget; and the number of staff, events, and volunteers." Engagement benchmarking, the newer approach, "looks at how your alumni feel about you and how those feelings influence action."[5] Engagement benchmarking is more costly than operational benchmarking, but many institutions think it's worth the extra expenditure for the value of the information they receive.

ENGAGEMENT

The ICARS measures of success (numbers of attendees, volunteers and donors) all hinge on engagement. But while we know that engaging alumni *anywhere* is more than just the numbers of bodies present, we also know that defining and measuring engagement is difficult.

- **Demonstrate that what you're doing is effective.** Analysis "gave us national averages we could compare ourselves to" instead of relying on anecdotal evidence, says Helen Murphy, director of alumni affairs at St. Francis Xavier University.

- **Balance out the viewpoints.** "When you have a board of directors with all the same personal experiences, they tend to think that's what everyone wants," says Susan Linders-Anderson, director of alumni and parent relations at California State University, Chico. "Benchmarking allows you to demonstrate when that's not the case."

- **Deploy limited resources more effectively.** Benchmarking can make you more strategic, says Jason Coolman, director of alumni affairs at the University of Waterloo. "It helps when we make a pitch for an increase in budget that we can show it's something that will produce results."

- **Provide data points for decision making.** "We were looking at the frequency of our alumni magazine and trying to determine what was standard," reports Sue Rees, alumni relations manager at the University of Ulster. Survey results allowed Rees to tell her board that the majority of institutions send out an alumni magazine twice a year.

- **Demonstrate responsiveness to alumni needs and feedback.** After conducting an alumni attitude survey, Linders-Anderson says, California State University, Chico, responded by telling alumni, "This is what you told us, and this is what we're going to do because of that."

- **Replace misperceptions with facts.** "I once had a vice president who said, 'The problem is that all you do is athletic events,'" says Joe Flanagan, director of alumni services at St. Bonaventure University. "Because I had the data, I was able to show that actually only 10 percent of our events are related to athletics."

- **Connect alumni with meaningful opportunities.** "Because our survey wasn't anonymous, we were able to follow up with those people who indicated interest in continuing education, for example," says Coolman.

- **Gain a seat at the leadership table.** "We already have the ear of our president, but I'm not sure every alumni office does. By collecting this kind of information, you can get the attention of higher-ups," says Murphy.

- **Improve your performance.** "When we started participating in [CASE's] benchmarking survey, it made us look at how we actually record data. We did it badly in some instances. So now we've changed the way we record data income and expenditures on events," says Rees. This type of change helps both in planning and reporting.

Adapted from Maura King Scully, "The Top 10 Reasons to Benchmark," CURRENTS 36 (January 2010): 20.

Since 2007, Ray Satterthwaite, founder and owner of Engagement Analysis and executive director of advancement at Ashbury College, has developed another way of thinking about alumni involvement and proposes new ways to measure the effectiveness of alumni relations. With more than 20 years of experience in advancement at Canadian institutions, Satterthwaite is encouraging others to prepare for a new form of internal benchmarking.[6]

"Many times there are no visible and ready metrics in alumni relations," begins Satterthwaite. "The challenge I always found was being consistent with what and how we measure." For example, outputs, such as attendance numbers, are just one type of measure. Perhaps more important is what drove the alumnus to participate in the program in the first place. Does effective marketing, for example, increase engagement?

Satterthwaite cautions that data can be skewed by alumni attitudes, and it is difficult to have a single objective lens from which to interpret results. How do you compensate for the lack of clarity? Satterthwaite goes straight to the alumni in a survey that tries to separate alumni attitudes toward the *institution* from their feelings about an *event*. Satterthwaite's survey includes 12 groups of "drivers," or questions, testing an alumnus's propensity to care about alma mater, grouped under the categories of reputation, relationship and result. (See figure 2.1.)

These 12 engagement drivers—including academic experience, reputation pride, reputation awareness, communication (propensity to read email), participation, involvement opportunity, awareness of need ("I know what the direction and priorities are"), involvement action, support level and activities—are all correlated to lifetime giving, according to Satterthwaite. "As engagement goes up, giving goes up. Engaged alumni are also high on the *net promoter* score, a key for international brand awareness."

TIP

Benchmarking involves collecting multiple institutions' data on an issue of common interest, viewing your own institution's performance over time and from the perspectives of what your peer and industry leaders are doing, and then using the perspective gained for internal continuous improvement. What it's *not* about: rankings, arms races and beauty contests.

Benchmarking questions might include:

- How do we compare to the whole population/ our peer group/industry leaders/individual institutions of interest?

- How "different" are we? Are we different for the "right" reasons?

- Are the others doing something we are not or are they doing the same things but doing them better to get their different results?

- Who do we look at for best practices?

- How have we changed over time?

From Judith Kroll, "What Does Successful Alumni Relations Look Like?" CASE report, June 2010

FIG. 2.1 | ENGAGEMENT DRIVERS

REPUTATION

Academic Experience	=	I was very satisfied with my academic experience.
Extra-curricular Experience	=	I valued my extracurricular experience.
Reputation Awareness	=	I am aware of the school's current reputation.
Reputation Pride	=	I am proud of my association with the school.

RELATIONSHIP

Alumni Communication	=	I keep informed of what is going on at the school.
Alumni Participation	=	I often participate in the activities of the school.
Involvement Opportunity	=	There are many interesting ways for me to be involved.
Involvement Action	=	I am willing to get involved in the school's activities.

RESULTS

Awareness of Case	=	I know what the school's needs are.
Impact of Giving	=	I know what the school's needs are.
Donor Participation	=	I support my school regularly.
Donor Level	=	I support my school to the best of my capacity.

Responses from 200,000 people, collected over the course of two and a half years, continue to validate Satterthwaite's model. "The responses are all in a pool, and we see which groups are responding in a like way; we are connecting responses together," he explains.

"It's not about how many reunions you have, it's about the feelings alumni have," he adds. "When it comes to international alumni engagement, I'm finding that with almost all the institutions that I've studied, international alumni are more engaged than the average alumni from their country."

Dr. Peter Brunner, the head of alumni relations at UTH-Zurich, agrees: "Emotions for our university are proportional to the distance they [alumni] are from the campus."[7]

Conversely, in Boston, for example, Tufts alumni are engaged and aware of what the university is doing, but they tend to suffer a bit on participation because the school is local. Thus there are some gains and some losses, depending on geography, and the job at Tufts is to determine how to gain in both situations with domestic and international alumni. International alumni may not be aware of the fundraising priorities of their alma mater but they are aware of the events. This awareness is measured by the 12 drivers presented in Satterthwaite's analysis.

"Affinity can happen between institutions, demographically (local vs. international) and by profession," concludes Satterthwaite. "We can slice and dice [the data] in many ways. We can ask, 'Are the international law alumni (or alumni of professional schools, or any other segment) more or less engaged?'"

Assessing Effectiveness

How do universities in different regions go about evaluating pieces of their international alumni programs?

Cambridge University

Cambridge University describes its current level of evaluation as an active "work in progress." For many years, Cambridge had a small alumni staff delivering services, so measurement did not exist at the level of some peer institutions. But Nathalie Walker, head of alumni relations, and Molly Peoples, alumni relations manager of networks and volunteers, are now looking at a closer application of metrics across the program. "Historically we may have promoted group membership but we were not sharing the data [of new members]. Today, we want to encourage communication and a process," states Walker.[8]

Walker and the Office of Alumni Relations started expanding their evaluations by asking a limited number of questions of their alumni through surveys. Responses helped Cambridge learn whether alumni were interested in getting involved and with which alumni groups they would want to affiliate. "We want to now ask more systematic questions to get more data on the alumni," Walker continues.

> **SURVEY QUESTION**
>
> Based on your relationship with the University of Cambridge, which do you most affiliate with?
>
> - My college
> - My faculty
> - My university
>
> Answers allowed young alumni to say "this is what I care about" and, in turn, help alumni relations identify new ways of relating.

Cambridge has employed the tactics from Satterthwaite's Engagement Analysis and surveyed their young alumni (graduates from the last 10 years) across all their colleges. Results of the survey showed young alumni affiliate with the faculty of specific departments. Based on this analysis, Cambridge can deploy more tactics that connect alumni back to their academic departments as the university tries to achieve a higher level of engagement among its alumni. Cambridge can also begin to benchmark their graduate responses across colleges.

Additionally, since a large percentage of Cambridge graduates affiliate with a specific department, one would make the case that the focus should be on the most popular degree subjects. And with some faculty crossing over colleges, it may be the college, the faculty or the university as a whole that would make a connection to alumni. Satterthwaite's findings at Cambridge show older alumni affiliating with the university as a whole, but in recent years, the deans of the colleges have become more aggressive in meeting individual alumni throughout events and cultivation opportunities.

Cambridge also plans to review the vice-chancellor's travel. In the past, Cambridge development office's international fundraiser organized events. Today, the alumni relations staff can send out recruitment mailing to different constituent groups and track new members and likely new donors. Walker says that the alumni office knows the vice-chancellor's travel schedule for the next 14 months. "In general, it's one of the things that we are trying to make more out of from an alumni perspective," Walker adds.

University of British Columbia

The University of British Columbia (UBC) has begun an institutional global plan, and alumni relations is actively contributing their pieces to it. About 20,000 UBC alumni self-report that they are volunteering for alma mater. The university alumni relations' goal is to double the number of active alumni by 2015. To achieve this goal, says UBC Director of Alumni Relations Barney Ellis-Perry, alumni relations decided to focus on three areas:

1. Foster the growth and development of UBC's alumni communities
2. Create access for all alumni to a ready network of peers and the UBC learning environment
3. Equip UBC students to make the most of their UBC networks

FIG. 2.2 | UBC'S ALUMNI DASHBOARD

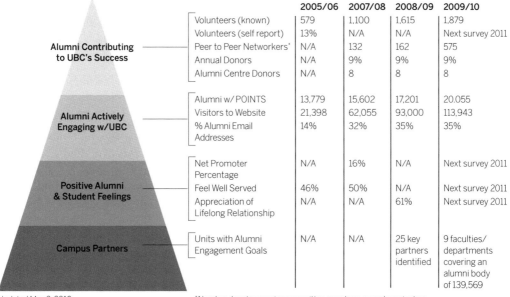

		2005/06	2007/08	2008/09	2009/10
Alumni Contributing to UBC's Success	Volunteers (known)	579	1,100	1,615	1,879
	Volunteers (self report)	13%	N/A	N/A	Next survey 2011
	Peer to Peer Networkers*	N/A	132	162	575
	Annual Donors	N/A	9%	9%	9%
	Alumni Centre Donors	N/A	8	8	8
Alumni Actively Engaging w/UBC	Alumni w/ POINTS	13,779	15,602	17,201	20,055
	Visitors to Website	21,398	62,055	93,000	113,943
	% Alumni Email Addresses	14%	32%	35%	35%
Positive Alumni & Student Feelings	Net Promoter Percentage	N/A	16%	N/A	Next survey 2011
	Feel Well Served	46%	50%	N/A	Next survey 2011
	Appreciation of Lifelong Relationship	N/A	N/A	61%	Next survey 2011
Campus Partners	Units with Alumni Engagement Goals	N/A	N/A	25 key partners identified	9 faculties/ departments covering an alumni body of 139,569

Updated May 3, 2010

*Number denotes reunion committee members, award nominators, branch reps and active presidential connectors

UBC uses an Alumni Dashboard (see figure 2.2) to track their effectiveness in achieving greater alumni engagement and in creating increased opportunities for student-alumni involvement as well as for more campus partnerships. Cumulatively, the dashboard represents the overall success of UBC's alumni relations with respect to its annual goals. The dashboard measures engagement in a number of ways, from number of volunteers (known and self-reported) to website visits, to alumni with "points"—for example, a graduate who buys a bookstore item, attends an event, mentors a student or engages in other defined proactive efforts. The staff also measure alumni engagement through "peer-to-peer networkers." As Tanya Walker, UBC's alumni affairs senior alumni relations manager, explains, "We hope our thought leaders can influence other peers to get involved. We want them to say to fellow alumni, 'Your time and talent will be well spent, and getting involved provides you access and opportunities to influence.'"[9]

There are a variety of ways to measure engagement and UBC has chosen to track personal involvement and attendance as a positive measure. Satterthwaite would caution against assuming that someone who attends an event had a positive experience.

University of Toronto

When asked about the readiness of their international relations program to adapt and change over time, Jeremy Woodall looks to the next five to 10 years and points to two priorities. "We have an adaptable program since our focus is on fostering alumni communities. Our [first] goal is to attract alumni and keep them engaged. We try to keep up with local alumni expectations."[10]

The second priority is related to development. "One of our long-term goals is to change the ways our alumni think about regular sustained annual giving in Asia. We are working to cultivate a new appreciation in younger alumni groups that our international communities have a tremendous potential to impact change. They really can advance the institution's international programming through gifts as small as 500 Hong Kong dollars." U of T will be tracking engagement and participation by younger alumni closely in the next five years.

MAINTAINING ENGAGEMENT

No matter how it's measured, engagement is the key to a strong and successful alumni relations program, overseas or at home.

Findings from the 2009 ICARS on correlations between alumni relations and "success" measures indicated the following:

- To increase the number of attendees, institutions should put on more events (rather than making existing events bigger) and connect with potential attendees through email or e-newsletters.

- To increase the number of volunteers, institutions should connect with them through email or e-newsletters and should have a website and a frequently published magazine.
- To increase the number of donors, "be prepared for the long haul, years of asking and years of having an e-newsletter and a dedicated website" and a frequently published magazine.[11]

ICARS, of course, defines success in terms of the numbers of attendees, volunteers and donors; Satterthwaite's model measures engagement in other ways. Institutions need to consider budgets, staffing levels, communications plans and other strategic considerations to sustain optimal levels of engagement in order to achieve their own definition of *success*.

Communications

Market Research

In order to build and maintain a successful program, "institutions need to know why and how their alumni want to engage with them," points out Elizabeth Scarborough, CEO of SimpsonScarborough, a market research and strategy firm based in the United States.[12] "Research should be used to explore the factors that motivate international alumni to seek a relationship with their alma mater."

Scarborough offers a few reasons why alumni might want to make a connection:

- Do they hope to simply connect socially with friends and former professors?
- Do they hope to gain new knowledge that will support their career?
- Do they hope to resurrect the feeling of pride they felt as a student?
- Do they feel an altruistic tug to "give back"?

"The 'how' of engaging alumni is particularly important when working with international alumni," Scarborough continues. "In-person engagement opportunities are typically limited and the vast array of online or 'distance' activities need to be carefully identified to reveal the tools, tactics, and vehicles that will do the best job of building a connection despite the geographic chasm that may exist between the graduate and the physical campus. In a word, *research* is essential in building a successful program."

Surveys may not be able to solve all problems, "But good research can help institutions understand how to better connect with alumni. Information gleaned from surveys can help alumni professionals tweak programming and create events and opportunities that are more popular, more meaningful, and more successful at connecting alumni back to the institution."[13]

Social Media

Using social media to communicate with international alumni is standard practice among most institutions. Facebook accounts for the bulk of activity and more than 70 percent of Facebook users are based outside the United States.[14] Alumni relations and communications staffs are customizing Facebook pages and are creating Facebook groups to increase participation and ownership of regional alumni. Moreover, more and more individuals own smart phones and have ready access to social media from their hand-held devices. Communicating with alumni has never been easier, but what will be the new standards for social media and international alumni relations? Your institution's strategic communications plan should be nimble enough to allow for rapid changes in technology. According to Lisa Notter, director of advancement communications at Lewis University, and Michael Eck, new media and advancement communications project manager at Lewis University, the near future is about greater integration and personalization of social media. Facebook, Twitter, and LinkedIn accounts may be combined to bring ease of access and greater participation among users.[15] Just as Amazon.com tracks previous purchases to market future buying opportunities, web-based and mobile phone applications will be developed to attract and retain the affinity of international alumni. Does this pose some risks? Not initially; using technology is an effective, creative and collaborative way of reaching out to others, tracking data and surveying the interests of alumni. But it is not low cost (see discussion below under "Services and Staffing").

Andy Shaindlin, founder of Alumni Futures, shares another viewpoint about social media.[16] "I distinguish between 'communications' and 'engagement.' I think that social tools have a communications function (sending news and information), but their real long-term value is in engaging alumni. This often means giving them a platform for conversation or interaction and getting out of their way. Not talking, just listening. This is a fundamentally new and challenging paradigm for traditional communications pros."

> **TIP**
>
> In June 2010, CASE, in partnership with mStoner and Slover Linett Strategies, launched a survey on social media in advancement. More than 18,000 U.S. and international CASE members at independent schools, colleges and universities were asked to participate, and nearly 1,000 did so.
>
> Among the findings: The biggest challenges that are keeping institutions from doing more with social media are staffing, expertise, and funding.
>
> From Cheryl Slover-Linett and Michael Stoner, "Social Experiments: Results from CASE's inaugural survey of social media in advancement," CURRENTS 36 (November/December 2010): 32, 35.

The University of Auckland has asked international alumni to run alumni pages for the university's alumni association on local social networking sites. In Korea the university has an alumni page on Cy World, which is used by 95 percent of Koreans and is more popular there than Facebook. "The challenges are to ensure that our volunteers update the site with information on news and events and [that] it has links to our official university alumni website and our Facebook alumni page," says Auckland's Alumni Relations Manager Amanda Lyne.[17]

Determining which local social networking site is preferred by your alumni is the first step. If a site is easy to use, regularly accessible, and generally reputable, the challenges of having one more communications source to update may be worth the time and effort.

But most institutions, in Shaindlin's opinion, will be better served by picking and choosing three or four tools that alumni are already using and making clear to their audience that this is where the school's content currently lives online.

Scarborough agrees: "An institution should stay focused on strategy and goals, first; tools and tactics should stem from these. An example is the recent Spartan Sagas initiative at Michigan State. The university's brand centers on 'hardworking excellence.' To engage alumni, they sought to create a vehicle for hardworking Spartans who are making a difference in their communities and around the globe to share their stories with each other and the world. Hundreds of alumni ultimately shared their 'saga' on a web page that was designed to gather and disseminate their stories. Had the university created a web page that was not so centrally focused on their brand, it's unlikely they would be generating so much attention."

Ongoing Assessment

Keeping pace with developing technology is a challenge that will require institutions to continue to assess the best modes of communication. Beyond assessment must lie a willingness to learn and use new forms of communication.

At the Benenden School, one of the U.K.'s most prestigious independent schools, a major goal is the development of technology. The staff received a primer from the advertising world in the fall of 2009. Development Director Debra Price sought information about trends and future practices to help inform her thinking over the next five years. She was trying to find a fresh way for Benenden to connect with its students and young alumni, since young adults communicate more via social media. Additionally, Benenden wants to find ways to make older alumni comfortable with technology.[18]

To that end, Price and her department spent a day with one of Britain's biggest advertisers, asking how it uses e-communications to promote brands in Britain. This form of corporate cross-training helped Price learn what is possible in the coming years, valuable information to share with Benenden's information technology department. Price recounts the day: "We had an afternoon together and we were part of a presentation about best and worst practices of e-communications and using technologies of the future. We discussed which cutting-edge industries are using e-communications and, now, we are working on reviewing our own communications plan." Price says that this learning experience, followed by her own internal communications review, has led her to believe that some efforts will never move to e-communications. "Some of the pieces will remain hard copy. These are precious."

In the next three years Benenden expects to formalize other alumni networks in New Zealand and Australia and will increase its work in India and Russia. Electronic invitations and other means of communication are the most economically viable and efficient way to support the school's expansion plans.

At the American School in Japan, the development and alumni relations staff is developing a strategic communications plan for the school. Staff predicts an overhaul of many services and programs and expects to redefine target audiences. "For the last two years, we focused on using social media, and we were one of the first schools to use this," says Andrea Booth, ASIJ alumni relations officer.[19] "However, in a year from now, I bet we look a lot different." In addition to changes to traditional communications channels, such as moving class agent contact information and class letters from ASIJ's print magazine, the *Ambassador*, to sections on its online community, the staff continues to scale back resources. ASIJ will not send staff to events and will reduce the number of receptions in the United States from four to one per year. Aiming for more strategic programs in recent years, ASIJ has focused on e-communications and engaging local alumni and is using both the parent and the local alumni community to bring speakers to campus for a student/alumni speaker series. This is an economical way to add value to programs.

Budgeting and Resource Allocation

Budgeting

International alumni relations programs attract alumni, parents, prospective students and potential donors, but why is the international alumni relations program usually perceived to be underfunded—especially when considering the financial realities of planning events overseas and coping with fluctuating exchange rates, an environment that can quickly change, and a variety of cultural norms? There is a clear argument for spending 95 percent of the central alumni relations budget on services and programs that cater to 95 percent of the alumni populations residing in the home country, but when the efforts of the international alumni relations program provide direct benefit to so many other campus departments, why shouldn't budgets be shared?

This is something to discuss across the campus during the planning cycle for an upcoming fiscal year. If the parents program office is not going to program internationally but there is an expectation that all parents of current students are invited to international events, is there a way to share the ultimate costs incurred by alumni relations? Do the annual fund or major gift areas contribute a set amount of money each year to the alumni relations operating fund so events can continue to be sponsored and staff can continue to travel to meet with alumni?

Finally, will advancement operations send a clear sign of commitment to their international alumni relations program by designating a shared international budget for the offices who most likely engage with international alumni? Externally we may be sending strong signals that "we are all one," but internally can we commit to making sure we have the resources it takes to sustain our expectations for future growth and development?

Services and Staffing

Sustaining effective programs and communications is not a "low cost" endeavor. According to Andy Shaindlin,[20] the personalization of international alumni relations work has high overhead in terms of staff time. Individual attention to alumni and donors does not scale. Also, Shaindlin points out, integrating social tools into communications in general is an institution-wide priority that cannot be successfully executed by an alumni or development office acting on its own.

With resource allocation in mind, the United World College Southeast Asia has been reviewing the menu of services offered to alumni. The alumni relations staff members have researched other alumni programs online, talked to alumni and mapped out what services they want to provide. Today, although they wish to continually add to their program of services, their primary focus is to maintain and enhance the current services (regional reunions, web-based communities, publications and a mentorship program). UWCSEA would need another staff member to help with the increased flow of communications into and out of the office before introducing new initiatives.[21]

A recent white paper, "Use of Technology for Development and Alumni Relations Among CASE Members,"[22] presented results from a comprehensive survey of 89 independent schools and 268 higher education institutions. The paper, which "explores the role of 'advancement-enabling' technology in helping institutions meet the challenges of engaging constituents and attracting private support," looks at how effective online communities and social media were in raising participation and support from alumni, parents and friends, among other support groups. An important point to consider is that institutions can't sacrifice staffing if they want to make the most of new technologies and communications techniques—although many institutions appear to be "under-resourcing":

> Several findings in the research underscore the theme that a lack of staff resources prevents advancement professionals from both functioning more effectively in general, and also from leveraging technology to a greater degree. One-half of advancement professionals consider a lack of staff and financial resources to be a significant challenge, as do 38% of respondents at independent schools. Advancement professionals' primary barrier to using technology more effectively is a lack of staff to support their technology needs. The majority of advancement systems are primarily supported by the institution's central information technology department, which suggests that technology needs for advancement may not be appropriately resourced by the institution.[23]

The bottom-line message: Technology doesn't run itself. People are still the primary factors in the engagement process.

Collaboration

Collaboration goes beyond budgets and coordinating technology across campuses. There are many other avenues to campus buy-in—and support—for an international alumni relations program. In 2006, our Tufts World Day was designed specifically to expose a large number of domestic and international chapters to our pre-campaign celebration while also providing colleagues in admissions, study abroad offices and the parents program (all co-sponsors of World Day), to name a few, an opportunity to travel on behalf of the university, fulfill their own program needs and support a comprehensive and strategic program.

In regard to collaboration, the four pillars of engagement (see figure 1.1) may be interpreted in several ways. For my international alumni relations planning, I am now using the pillars as a barometer by which to measure Tier 1, Tier 2 and Tier 3 regional chapters for Tufts University. Tier 1 regions produce a proportionally high number of international applications for the first year class, and the undergraduate admissions office deems these regions a priority; Tier 1 regions also have a Tufts-affiliated study-abroad center or may host centers for Tufts academic programs or partnerships with at least one of our schools; finally, Tier 1 regions have a robust and active chapter community of alumni from all schools, parents and friends. Fellow advancement officers will usually find more than one opportunity to visit Tier 1 regions.

The four pillars of engagement may also be used internally across campus when thinking about staffing, resources and budgetary planning for international alumni relations. Above, the discussion on budgets proposes a collaborative budgeting process that could pool resources to support overall institutional international outreach. What if we added resources from the enrollment management and academic sides of the house? Who would ultimately decide how much and for what purposes? An exercise like this alone would inspire immediate dialogue and introspection about the international aims of the institution.

The CASE/SunGard white paper also concludes a need for more institution-wide collaboration between alumni relations and development, advancement and central information technology departments, as well as advancement and other departments such as enrollment management.[24]

Ideally, wouldn't a centralized tracking system for all international outreach and engagement (from admissions, alumni, parents, sabbatical schedules, study-abroad, to name a few) be an efficient and transparent way of measuring progress?

CONCLUSION

Whether your work is based in Asia, North America or Europe, efforts to identify, attract and engage alumni through creative systems of communication and programming are increasing each year. Technology today creates easy-to-use, cost-effective and mobile forms of staying in touch with alumni. But should it replace the face-to-face meetings? Does "breaking bread" still remain important in some cultures? Every situation requires a different approach.

As advancement professionals, we will continue to learn from each other and our experiences both at home and abroad. By doing so, we add value to the profession, to our work and to the experiences of our alumni. As one head of alumni relations in Asia feels: "We learn a lot of global trends from American schools, but we also want to 'leap frog' a new generation (of alumni) in areas of technology. How we revamp the web site and give alumni a new email address (is strategic). We need to continue to invest in the future."[25]

ENDNOTES

1. Judith Kroll, "What Does Successful Alumni Relations Look Like?" CASE report, June 2011, 1.

2. Ibid.

3. Ibid., 6, 10.

4. "Ready, Set, Benchmark," CURRENTS 36 (January 2010): 25.

5. Maura King Scully, "Are We There Yet? Alumni Professionals Have Made Great Strides in Proving the Value of Their Work," CURRENTS 36 (January 2010): 18.

6. Unless otherwise indicated, quotations from Satterthwaite in the following paragraphs taken from telephone interview with author, Nov. 26, 2010.

7. Peter Brunner, interview with author, Oct. 22, 2009, at IARU Alumni Directors Summit, Yale University.

8. Quotations from Nathalie Walker from email to author, Feb. 9, 2011.

9. Tanya Walker, telephone interview with author, Sept. 14, 2010.

10. Jeremy Woodall, telephone interview with author, July 13, 2009. At the time of this interview, Woodall was at U of T's advancement office in Hong Kong. He is now director of the University of Oxford's China office.

11. Kroll, "What Does Successful Alumni Relations Look Like?" 8.

12. Elizabeth Scarborough, email interview with author, Dec. 12, 2010. Other Scarborough quotations in this chapter are also from this interview.

13. Erin Peterson, "Know Your Market," CURRENTS 34 (October 2008): 27.

14. Information from *Leveraging Social Media to Transform Alumni Communications*, CASE Online Speaker Series, June 17, 2010, presented by Lisa Notter and Michael Eck, Lewis University.

15. Ibid.

16. Andy Shaindlin, email to author, Dec. 8, 2010.

17. Amanda Lyne, email to author, Nov. 16, 2010.

18. Debra Price, telephone interview with author, June 10, 2009.

19. Andrea Booth, telephone interview with author, June 10, 2009.

20. Shaindlin interview, Dec. 8, 2010.

21. David Shepherd and Brenda Whately, telephone interview with author, June 3, 2009.

22. Isurus Market Research and Consulting, "Use of Technology for Development and Alumni Relations among CASE Members," report prepared for CASE and SunGard Higher Education, July 2010.

23. Ibid., 5.

24. Ibid., 8.

25. Choo Soo Tsei, telephone interview with author, July 13, 2009.

CHAPTER 3

MAKING THE CASE
Best Practices in Organizing and Managing International Alumni Programs

Can we sustain chapters?

What would be our model for self-sustaining groups?

What is the best way to engage alumni with students? How do you best use the on-campus resources of your faculty?

Can "community" be accomplished and sustained with electronic communications and social media tools such as Facebook and LinkedIn?

When looking at ways to engage alumni, staff at schools and universities can consider many different ways to organize and manage an international alumni relations program. Models range from staff-driven to volunteer driven, regional to virtual. Educational institutions also need to think about what sort of programming they'll offer to engage their overseas alumni. In this chapter, we'll look at best practices in four areas: managing from a distance, student-alumni programming, programming with faculty and signature programs.

One way to decide how a program will be run is by determining how to work with alumni abroad to build community and support for each other and for their alma mater. Organizational models for alumni groups vary by an institution's size, geography and constituency. Often, the high cost of travel and the opportunity costs of time and human resources can be important factors in this decision, prompting schools, colleges and universities to rethink their approaches and ask some of the questions posed above.

Additionally, as part of an annual evaluation process, as you are aligning financial resources to programs, you should ask these key questions:

- Is our institution in the position to sustain the current model of alumni groups in the coming year, the next three years, and into the next campaign?
- Can the goals we set for our international alumni relations program be achieved by involving different relationships across key regions?

Exploring these questions will help anticipate and plan for any necessary changes. Each institution will answer these questions in a distinct way.

When thinking about student-alumni programming, independent schools face different considerations than do institutions of higher education—and each independent school has its own particular challenges to meet that are as individual as the school itself. In the next major group of case studies, "Student-Alumni Programming," we'll explore what some independent schools are doing to connect their students with alumni and their alumni with students.

Additionally, we'll look at how colleges, universities and business schools are trying to make these same connections. Most institutions would agree that the sooner your "alumni-in-training" learn of the benefits of membership in an alumni association, the better. For all students, the benefits of getting to know international alumni translate to better internships, jobs, mentoring opportunities and assistance while traveling and studying abroad. The second section in this chapter will introduce several examples of how universities are encouraging their alumni abroad to become active partners with students seeking assistance and advice.

The next section will examine two business schools' approaches to building community with current students and international alumni.

Finally, we'll look at some signature programs—those special efforts that have worked well for institutions' international alumni relations programs.

The examples you'll find throughout this chapter provide a variety of models and approaches across independent schools, colleges, universities and business schools. Some examples are elaborated to illustrate what is driving their decisions and how demographics and resources may change current practices over time.

MANAGING FROM A DISTANCE

Independent Schools

United World College of South East Asia

The United World College of South East Asia (UWCSEA) follows the regional model. It holds events in areas around the world in cities with high numbers of alumni and enough interested volunteers willing to help with programs—a fool-proof combination for the success of regional events. (A measure of "enough" I've often employed is whether there are at least 200 to 250 alumni in a given city, although parents provide valuable support for regional endeavors and should be encouraged to participate.)

Founded in 1971 in Singapore, UWCSEA boasts well over 200,000 alumni. It held its first London Reunion in January 2007. The event, which attracts large numbers of its alumni in the U.K., experienced significant growth between 2007 and 2009, start-ing out with 190 alumni at the first reunion and growing to just under 300 in 2009.

In Singapore, an annual event is aimed primarily at recent UWCSEA gradu-ates who return to the country during their December breaks at their various universities. In 2010, UWCSEA added reunions in Mumbai, New York City, San Francisco and Jakarta.

UWCSEA's approach, established with its London program, is to bear the costs of each reunion and to organize the events itself. The office asks for guid-ance from alumni regarding local arrangements and logistics. As its regional program expands, UWCSEA hopes to have teams of volunteers in each city to handle more of the reunion program planning and details. UWCSEA has even been practicing in its own backyard. The school started a program in Singapore to recruit volunteers to help with a one-year planning effort in advance of its 30-20-10 Reunion Program (inviting graduates from 30, 20 and 10 years out), which is held locally on campus.

> **TIP**
>
> - Hold annual reunions in major cities with high concentrations of alumni.
> - Bear the cost of the reunions and organize the events—but get eager volunteers to help.

Phillips Exeter Academy

The alumni association at Phillips Exeter Academy, located in Exeter, New Hampshire, is more than 100 years old. Alumni volunteers were first engaged as admissions volunteers: interviewers, recruiters and resources for prospective students. Alumni events soon followed.

Exeter has more than 50 regional associations worldwide. On average, the school's alumni association sponsors more than 50 events per year. The oldest regional association was started in the 1960s in London by a former resident of Massachusetts who had been involved in Exeter's alumni associations in New York City and Boston. He saw an opportunity to organize in London and, with transferable experience, was a successful president of the Exeter London regional association for more than 20 years. The London group was the only international chapter for some time and remains the largest international alumni base for Exeter.

TIP

Train your advancement staff in the customs of areas outside your home country.

After London came Seoul, Bangkok, Hong Kong and Tokyo. As Exeter's international student population from Asia is rising, so too are those alumni numbers. Korean students make up the school's largest student group from Asia. Alumni in Seoul are interested in the same type of alumni activities as those occurring in New York City and Boston. Exeter does not sponsor a formal training for regional leaders but tries to makes its international strategy "seamless to our domestic strategy," says one administrator, in explaining why the school maintains its Western orientation.[1] Their approach to working with alumni from around the world is the same. The difference is that Exeter has brought in cultural experts to train the advancement staff in the customs and norms of areas outside the United States.

'Iolani School

Some schools have a "sister city" for alumni efforts outside the local area.

"If there is any chapter loosely defined [for our school], it will be Japan," states Val Iwashita, 'Iolani headmaster.[2] The school, located in Honolulu, has 1,840 students in grades K–12 and is a day school: parents of 'Iolani students must be residents of Hawaii. Most of 'Iolani's international alumni reside in Japan and other areas of Asia, and Iwashita and his staff focus on Tokyo as a base for regional events. The 'Iolani Alumni Gumi, or local association in Japan, is in contact with an average of 50 alumni in greater Tokyo, ranging from the class of 1964 to the class of 2006. Their annual dinner in December is their signature regional event, and in 2010, the group enhanced the holiday social with a drive to raise money and collect used clothing and new toys for a shelter for abused and neglected children.[3] With the 150th anniversary of 'Iolani in 2013, the school has an opportunity to capitalize on building a stronger relationship between the island campus and its overseas alumni. Even though there are alumni events occurring in cities such as San Francisco, Seattle and New York City, the Tokyo-based Gumi stand out among the rest as alumni inspired to replicate the community activities of the main campus experience in Honolulu.

'Iolani also relies on parents to help build these relationships. "We have identified families with the strongest connection. For us, it's a matter of data gathering and being sensitive to the relationships," says Iwashita. "Alumni and parents refer others to us (both local and abroad) who may be helpful in sustaining the well-being of the school's reputation and financial interests."

Since primary and secondary schools involve parents in the educational experience, it is common for alumni offices to include family of current and former students in their alumni "numbers" and databases. Family members of current students organize on campus and abroad in efforts to build relationships with the school and other constituents. Ideally, it is desirable to have their involvement extend well beyond graduation.

International School of Kuala Lumpur

Regional events will often require the guidance and assistance of a school's alumni director. When Toni Mullen attended the International School of Kuala Lumpur (ISKL) reunions around the world, she prepared a slideshow depicting the history of ISKL with highlights of students' campus experience. The slides included defining moments from each decade of the years related to the reunion attendees and information about how ISKL changed over the years. Mullen, who served as the director of alumni affairs at ISKL from 2005 to 2011, included a key picture for the reunion group (either a group picture or something emblematic to their era) and made copies of it for reunion guests. As another way of saying thank you, Mullen also presented alumni ID cards as a gift to each attendee and, after the reunion, sent IDs to those guests who registered late.[4]

> **TIP**
>
> Look to family members of current and former students to build relationships that support the school abroad. Keep parents involved beyond their students' graduation.

Alumni cohorts from the mid-1970s are active five-year reunion groups. These alumni, who are in their 50s, have been organizing their own reunions over the past decades. Recently, many have returned to Kuala Lumpur—some for the first time since the late 1960s and early 1970s. These alumni actively encourage more alumni to reconnect to ISKL through the ISKL website or through the "official" IKSL alumni group on Facebook. Other decades have taken their lead from the 1960s/1970s group and are organizing their own alumni gatherings worldwide. While director, Mullen either attended these events or sent an "ISKL in a Box" to share with the attendees. The "box" typically contained the alumni ID cards, the slide-show, alumni bumper stickers, magnets and some gifts from the ISKL Booster Hut (which is run by the Parent-Teacher Association).

With each alumni group or council having its own personality and protocol (in Tokyo, alumni pay at the door for events; in Houston and recently in Sydney, alumni events were hosted by an alumnus from the 1970s), ISKL believes the easiest way to plan events is to use private homes or a private club setting. This method eliminates the difficulty of renting spaces in large cities, and catering may be far more economical. Plus, this allows for more intimate gatherings where alumni from across the decades can quickly make connections and share their stories and memories.

ISKL creates other opportunities for alumni to gather. When an ISKL administrator or counselor goes on the road, ISKL will sponsor an alumni gathering one evening during their trip. Additionally, the head of school will meet with alumni each time he or she makes a trip. These efforts enhance ongoing and direct contact by the alumni affairs office.

Mullen also took advantage of alumni councils to help maintain regional alumni programs for ISKL. Class agents represent their graduation years and, together, they make up an alumni council, or chapter, for their particular region. ISKL's alumni numbers include former students, parents, extended families, and faculty. Mullen used email and social networking through Facebook and Linked In ("ISKL Career Connection") to keep in touch with alumni on a daily basis and to expand the opportunities for alumni to share their contact information with the school as well as available jobs. Class agents also used email to communicate but were concerned primarily with reunion outreach and activities by and for their classmates.

Mullen orchestrated this volunteer base of more than 270 class agents around the world who assisted the school with outreach to classmates and help organize events. Alongside alumni, interested parents of both current and past students serve as class agents and can help with particular events and facilitate the registration of alumni parents.

American School in Japan

Founded in 1902, the American School in Japan (ASIJ) is one of the oldest private

> **TIP**
>
> • Be creative in your approach to regional events—not all need to be staffed. Send "event boxes" to show support and encourage ties to alma mater.
>
> • Holding events in private homes or clubs eliminates the difficulty of renting space in a large city and allows for more intimate gatherings where alumni can share memories and make connections.

schools in the Asia-Pacific region. More than half the student body holds U.S. passports, and its U.S.-based alumni and current students top 6,000.

ASIJ's class program for alumni is organized by volunteer class agents. Volunteers are given a checklist of ideas and a comprehensive "Class Reunion Organizing Survival Guide" to aide in planning.[5]

For their U.S. alumni and students, ASIJ once tried to facilitate an ambassador program whereby alumni could self-identify themselves as hosts or resources in their cities. It was hard to manage and never gained much ground, says a member of the ASIJ staff. "The same goes for the career mentoring program," concurs another staff member. Alumni sign up initially, but the "problem with a school our size [is that] we don't have a critical mass. ... Even if we get 1 to 2 percent to sign up, it is still not enough," he adds.[6]

Altogether, ASIJ is trying to be more proactive in facilitating the students' networking to afford more internship opportunities. Communicating with alumni about these opportunities is at the top of the list with the staff.

ASIJ relies heavily on new technology to maintain contact and engagement, organize events and handle communications. With more than 7,000 alumni in the United States, but only one active alumni chapter—in Tokyo—and an alumni council, the school is running more of a communications program than a chapter program, says ASIJ Alumni Relations Officer Andrea Booth.[7] ASIJ also has about 1,000 alumni in Japan, with 360 in the greater Tokyo area. The school's alumni database includes alumni and alumni parents, and the school retains both postal and electronic contact information on file.

Communication is largely electronic. A monthly e-newsletter goes to all alumni worldwide. The letter tries to provide a balance between news on campus and news abroad. Newsletters and the alumni magazine, the *Ambassador* (published twice a year and made available online), focus on alumni achievements. The magazine also features profiles of alumni as well as written work by students. In 2009, when the school's target of restricted fundraising was "green" themes, alumni in "green" professions were profiled in each issue. Most recently, Booth uses Twitter every day to share snippets about alumni activities and events. By mid-2011, ASIJ had gained about 700 followers since starting its Twitter account in 2008. This is just one of the new methods of communicating with alumni overseas.

> **TIP**
>
> - Comprehensive checklists and guides can help volunteers plan great reunions and other events.
> - Make sure you have a critical mass of graduates before undertaking a program overseas.
> - Social media and other electronic communication methods are efficient and cost-effective ways to stay in touch with alumni.

Benenden School

Another organizational approach is for a school to rely on self-sustaining chapters and initiatives. Benenden School in the U.K. uses this model for its international alumni relations efforts.

Founded in 1923, the Benenden School has about 525 students, representing more than 25 countries. For the past 50 years, the school has enrolled more students from India, Hong Kong and Malaysia than from any other areas.

"We have tried to develop as many self-contained groups as possible so efforts are not tied to staffing levels at Benenden," states Debra Price, the school's development director.[8] Benenden, a boarding school for girls, equips alumni leaders with the tools needed to stay in touch with the school and with one another. For example, alumni regional coordinators have direct access to a web-based membership database system. Regional coordinators can thus retrieve addresses, post events and change or update information about alumni whom they meet and/or are in touch with by virtue of their volunteer title. Benenden maintains the integrity of this information by requiring a school staff member to authorize each biographic or programmatic change to the system.

Benenden sponsors a Regional Coordinators Conference in London every other year. The school has divided the U.K. into 54 regions, and areas in the United States, Asia and Australia are also broken into geographic areas. At the one-day conference, for which British alumni leaders' travel costs are reimbursed, Benenden and its alumni leaders agree to "terms of engagement," that is, their policies of operations. "We have lots of examples of what's worked and what's happened," states Price. "We want to know what we can do to help the volunteers in their role. We have a job description for a regional coordinator, but we also recognize each region has its own character." An overall goal is to create a mechanism for building "senior-to-senior" or alumna-to-alumna contact. The school also uses the conference to strengthen communication ties from alumni back to the alumni office. In the end, the conference is an opportunity for the regional coordinators to share their unique regional experience with each other.

Benenden offers opportunities each year for all alumni to return to its campus in Kent, England, and to gather in London. These core programs—the 25th and 50th Reunions, the Alumni Day, and the London Christmas Carol Concert—are popular events. The 25th Reunion is held on campus and the 50th Reunion takes place in London. Alumni Day, held each May in Kent, is open to everyone. According to Price, the participation numbers increase every year. "In 2008 the Princess [Anne] came to speak at Seniors' Day, an annual alum event. That year was the 40th Anniversary of the Princess having left Benenden herself. Attendance for Seniors' Day more than doubled that year," says Price.

"We are relatively small, and we get 100 at the 50th reunion. This is a lot for us, especially when there were only 30 to 40 students a year back then. Every graduate from classes 50 years or older is invited every year."

Hong Kong is Benenden's most developed unit outside the U.K. "We have a lot of expats and Chinese families who live in Hong Kong, so it's not surprising that there is a lot of activity," says Price. A core program there is the popular Hong Kong work/experience intern program, which started in 2006. The program has been developed by alumni from Hong Kong interested in hosting 16- and 17-year-old Benenden students from around the world. Price puts students directly in contact with the alumni in Hong Kong, and students arrange for their summer or holiday internships. The program is especially popular among girls who live in Hong Kong.

Benenden's alumni bases in Bangkok, Kuala Lumpur and New York are increasing their activity with Benenden. The alumni in these cities are enthusiastic about belonging to a worldwide network of alumni and are offering to host regional dinners and socials on a regular basis.

Regional coordinators in New York City organize annual events, but because "most of our alumni there are transient," says Price, the group remains loosely organized by young alumni. "Whenever I or the headmistress travel to New York City we organize an event," she continues. "If we have 50 to 60 alumni in New York City, we can hope to meet at least half of them at the event. Alumni are on our fundraising board, and I encourage them to meet with fellow alumni in New York City when they are traveling to the States as another way to stimulate contact."

Simultaneously, the school is experiencing a greater interest in fundraising from the younger alumni in New York City. Price elaborates: "For years we did not go to New York City and did not contact New York City alumni. Once we did, about a year after we received gifts from alumni who had never made gifts before! As soon as we started spreading the news about Benenden's aspirations we had more interest. This is not similar to American fundraising, but this is a great new paradigm shift for us."

> **TIP**
>
> - Provide regional coordinators direct access to a web-based membership database. Focus on efficient and timely biographic updates to the alumni database and changes to event publicity.
>
> - Host regular training for the majority of alumni volunteers. Determine "terms of agreement" for all leaders.
>
> - Promote mentoring/internship programs and professional development among students only if a region has enough alumni to support such programs.
>
> - Promote a housing exchange: a listing of available housing opportunities organized by city and available online to students and/or alumni.

Young alumni are very helpful to Benenden seniors who seek housing after graduation. Seniors can use the school's web-based database to access alumni contact information in cities around the world.

Benenden has invested in its alumni volunteers. Price believes alumni are poised to lead the school to its centennial in 2024. They played a big role in the school's 75th anniversary celebration and other recent major events. Based on the level of active contribution for Benenden's 75th anniversary and on the growth of alumni support and programs in recent years, Price foresees more involvement than ever before.

Colleges and Universities

London School of Economics

The London School of Economics (LSE) is unique in that it attracts almost a majority of international students to its London campus and graduates students who will work and live in locations around the world. It is a campus primed for international alumni relations work, and in recent years, the institution has focused on this opportunity to build a network for itself beyond London.

LSE was founded in 1895 in the center of London's business district. Its approximately 9,000 full-time students and more than 800 part-time students come from about 140 countries (32 percent from the U.K., 19 percent from other European Union countries and 49 percent from other countries). The total number of addressable alumni tops 95,000. Forty-five percent of LSE alumni reside in the U.K.

LSE's entire advancement division includes five alumni relations officers and 12 other development officers. These 17 front-line professionals work with international alumni.

TIP

- Sponsor annual alumni leader training if you are starting a new program and have enough interest from alumni to build alumni groups quickly and effectively.

- Publish a chapter handbook and make it available online through an alumni intranet.

- Require alumni volunteers who have access to the database to sign a confidentiality agreement.

- Annually survey regional chapters at the same time every year.

- Don't concern your program with scale. Establish contact networks all over the world.

Although LSE is an established institution with a long heritage of a global community, its alumni association was just launched in 2005. Consequently, the staff members felt they needed to "play catch up" with some of their more active, larger alumni groups that had been autonomous for many years. They created a chapter handbook to build consistency across groups as well as to provide guidelines for planning events and electing officers. This initial handbook was primarily created for the international chapters as a means to coordinate activities and annually report back their progress each year. With a majority of alumni living outside the U.K., LSE staff has invested time in the handbooks. "We have much more of a business imperative to update [the handbook] because of the way our numbers work," explains Charlotte Armah, head of alumni relations.[9]

The handbook was published in 2005 and again in 2007 when LSE invited the alumni leaders to campus for a leadership forum. That was the last time the hard copy of the handbook was used. Today, LSE provides its resources online. The electronic forms for its guidelines are easy to update and access.

LSE has also created an electronic annual survey that all alumni association groups are required to complete. The survey is an assessment tool filed each year ahead of the leadership forum in the fall. Information about the history of the group, events held in the previous year and the group's perception of success and opportunities for improvement are described in the short survey.[10]

LSE has more than 50 established alumni regional groups outside of London. To maintain its footprint around the world, the alumni relations staff continues to augment its representation by adding more designated alumni contacts to its "contact networks." LSE has about 250 designated alumni contacts. In places such as Kenya and Bangladesh, where there are not enough alumni to warrant a formal chapter, more alumni are signing up for this role to represent LSE as an ambassador willing to provide information to prospective students and alumni relocating to their region.

Confidential information is regularly shared with alumni leaders, as they cannot properly fulfill their role without knowing who's who in a region: the personal and professional demographics are important indicators when planning events and recruiting volunteers and hosts. Like many institutions, LSE requires its alumni leaders to sign a confidentiality agreement outlining the proper (and improper) uses of the database information. (See figure 3.1.)

Indian Institute of Technology, Kanpur

The Indian Institute of Technology in Kanpur (IITK), one of several IITs in India, was founded in 1959 and is one of the top technological institutes in the country focusing on research in engineering and science.

Approximately 4,200 students study on the Kanpur campus. IITK's registrar counts 24,594 graduates since 1965. Of this number, 19,741, or 80 percent, are addressable alumni. Of the addressable alumni, 4,168, or 21 percent, live primarily in Australia, Bangladesh, Canada, France, Germany, Hong Kong, Japan, Malaysia, Singapore, the United Arab Emirates, the U.K., and the United States. In 2009, IITK's alumni relations responsibilities were headed up by Sanjeev Aggarwall, dean

FIG. 3.1 | LSE CONFIDENTIALITY AGREEMENT

LSE

Confidentiality agreement concerning personal data on LSE alumni

Between the London School of Economics, Office of Development and Alumni Relations and

LSE alumni club of _____ (country or region)

_____ Designated club representative

I understand that our organisation is holding data on LSE alumni which has been or will be sent to us from the data base maintained by the Office of Development and Alumni Relations at LSE.

This data is considered to be valuable property which I will safeguard. I agree that the sole purpose of this data is to expand the membership of our group and its activities and I agree to use this data only for this purpose. I agree not to use the data for any charitable fundraising, sales or marketing and I agree not to transfer any of this data to any commercial or non-commercial third party.

I agree to make all officers, board members or other leaders of my group aware of this policy.

I recognise the importance of a strong healthy central data base for LSE and I agree to help maintain the quality of the central LSE data base by encouraging alumni to email changes directly to the London office, by forwarding/faxing any dated correspondence concerning address changes, or by sending lists containing updates of addresses received since the last such communication.

Signed:_____

Title:
_____

Date:
_____

of resource planning and generation, who, along with four other staff members, led outreach and development programs for all alumni.

Aggarwall expressed deep interest in fostering relationships with everyone from undergraduate students to post-doctorate fellows. "We have contact information on 90 percent of the students who ever graduated from the prestigious undergrad program. That is about 10,000 (from 11,000 undergrads) and about half are located outside India in the USA, Europe and Australia."[11]

The IITK Alumni Association is the main body that organizes alumni chapters around the world. IITK has between 20 and 25 international alumni chapters. The largest are in major U.S. cities ("San Francisco is probably our largest chapter," says Aggarwall), and there is a very active group in Japan.

The alumni association encourages the formation of new groups. The election process of its governing board ensures international representation on its executive board. Alumni elect a president of the IITK alumni association as well as two vice presidents, one of whom is from the United States. An unusual feature of the IITK alumni membership body is that many faculty members are alumni and are, therefore, connected to the academic, student and advancement strategies for the institution. With the main alumni association office headquartered on the IITK campus, it is easy for faculty to participate in local functions and committee meetings.

In 2001, an IITK alumnus and the institution formed the IITK Foundation to encourage alumni donations to the IITK Annual Fund. The head of the foundation was the president of Chevron USA, and he, along with other influential IITK graduates, began raising money. The foundation, which is registered as a 501(c)3 nonprofit entity in the United States, provides tax benefits to alumni, parents and friends who make donations to IITK. There are now four IIT foundations in the United States.

> **TIP**
>
> - Ensure international alumni leaders have a voice on an alumni executive board.
>
> - Faculty who are alumni provide access and understanding about academic programs.
>
> - Regional alumni may have incentive to participate in annual giving through the establishment of a fund that provides local tax benefits.
>
> - Encourage a breadth of programs: social, professional, and events geared toward families.

All of IITK's chapters are organized by local alumni for mostly social and professional networking opportunities. It is common for groups in the United States to sponsor family picnics once a year. Aggarwall said he believes the IITK alumni chapters abroad are in good hands. "These are led by alumni who are very passionate about IIT-Kanpur. These alumni become our messengers."

Stanford University

Since 1991 Steve Suda, managing director of international principal gifts, a Stanford alumnus and former director of Stanford's international division, has met thousands of alumni abroad. Suda's early responsibilities included helping launch the international division and working as a development officer in Asia and Europe. By 1994, the university had decided to focus on Asia, and Suda was a primary development officer traveling abroad to meet alumni. He made his first trip to India in 1997, well before many U.S. universities had turned an eye toward that country. "I felt I had the luckier of assignments," recalls Suda.[12] During the next 10 years, Suda's contacts increased, as did interest in international alumni relations. Alumni abroad saw themselves as key players in the future of Stanford, and they wanted to build their own regional Stanford groups in their home countries and cities. This was a common theme among alumni of Stanford's seven schools, which were experiencing a growth in interest and support from alumni in Asia.

In 2007, Suda restructured the international division to serve as the coordinating body for international advancement efforts across the entire university. The work of the international alumni relations office, the Stanford alumni association and the professional schools, as well as efforts made by international development officers were tracked and shared on an ongoing basis as well as through quarterly meetings across the campus.

In preparation for the public phase of the $4.3 billion capital campaign, launched in October 2006, Suda also developed Stanford's International Development Council (IDC), whose members have the overarching goals of helping raise money and building alumni interest in their countries. Council members include 20 of Suda's closest contacts abroad, all of whom have knowledge about and experience with fundraising. Current members hail from Asia, Europe and the Middle East. The IDC has four goals:

1. Offer development advice and assistance. Members review prospect lists and advise staff on how to solicit prospective donors from their regions. Some make solicitations for Stanford.
2. Serve as advocates and ambassadors for the university.
3. Host or assist with regional events.
4. Review campaign messaging in materials (print and web) for cultural appropriateness. Members helped craft an international scholarship appeal so that the messaging was not as "U.S.-centric" as first designed.

TIP

- A designated person, staff and/or department coordinating all international outreach efforts across an institution benefits overall effectiveness, both internally and externally.

- Cross-training is essential. When one person has the sole responsibility for and knowledge of all international outreach efforts, there is the potential for a devastating impact on these efforts if that person leaves the institution.

- An International Development Council (IDC) serves as the tested and trusted alumni advisory body for international development and fundraising efforts.

Fundamentally, an international alumni relations program is about building relationships with others who share a mutual goal: to support and advance the well-being of an institution located outside their home country. Key decision-makers inside an institution are not going to be the only experts on other cultures, educational systems, local politics and sources of wealth. When the president, chancellor, vice president of advancement and others on campus think about the well-being of their relationships abroad, they may zero in on a group of advisers who share their interests in advancing the institution abroad. These "boards" and "councils" are proving to be successful groups for international alumni who are willing to share expertise and advice. They also provide a mechanism by which alumni relations and development officers can engage new volunteers, cultivate new donors and, in time, recognize the valuable contributions of these international partners.

When Suda travels to a country for the first time, he coordinates appointments with IDC members first in order to learn more about the region and have an orientation to the area from a trusted "insider." Learning what's important for Stanford to know about an area is one goal; another is to listen well to "what's on their mind" in order to be able to respond to their interests and follow up on their personal requests. It is a two-way street with this advisory board.

Stanford's IDC is visible recognition of what international alumni have accomplished working with Suda since 1991. Every member of the council has helped Suda in advancing Stanford's goals abroad. Some members have political connections, and others want to give their time. All are Stanford alumni and some are past or current parents of Stanford students. The members are appointed by a group within Suda's former office and their terms last the duration of the campaign. Members meet at regional events and are invited to special events back on the Stanford campus. Stanford's many academic programs around the world have helped the university build a great reputation and a great network. However, the IDC network is unique: "We have many international members on advisory boards at the university, but the IDC is the first instance of a specific focus on development and alumni relations," Suda clarifies.

Australian National University

The alumni relations profession took off in Australia in 1990. At that time, a push by the government for reforms at universities was seen as a challenge to institutional autonomy and academic freedom, and alumni rallied behind their alma maters when the institutions pushed back. The universities knew they had to maintain these valuable relationships with their alumni and capitalize on their involvement.

At about this same time, the government's "ability and willingness to fund the academic enterprise began to wane," and a three-tier fee system was instituted. From the university point of view, however, the new funding didn't pay for the "actual cost of the education provided."[13] Universities needed to look for other forms of support—namely, resources raised by new partners, including alumni, corporations and foundations. In order to meet these new challenges, the alumni relations staff at Australian National University (ANU) has had to be "extremely entrepreneurial," says Christine Keller Smith, alumni director at ANU from 2004 to 2009. "We do not do anything unless it is aligned to the university plans."[14]

With only two people making up the ANU alumni relations staff during her time as director, Keller Smith found she needed to be as strategic as possible with staff time and resources.

> **TIP**
>
> • Align staff and resources with goals for outreach and engagement.
>
> • Identify international alumni who have studied under government grants. They could be influential leaders in their countries and be good alumni to cultivate for future support.
>
> • Recognize cultural difference across the world. Some cultures desire more formal organization.

Part of her plan was to work with an alliance of 10 other Australian universities. Another was to align the alumni relations strategy with ANU's recruitment efforts.

"For example, we have a lot of government development grants we give to countries in need, and from there we do a lot of work in Indonesia and New Guinea," she explains. "Those alumni are sponsored to come to ANU. These are very influential people in their home country, and for us it's really important to have a relationship with these VIPs."

Upon arriving at ANU in 2004, Keller Smith's first priority was to build a database of alumni records, which she saw as an essential first step in being able to build relationships with ANU graduates. Using hard copies of graduation records, ANU began the project. Today, their database includes 76,000 total alumni, and 71 percent are addressable. Roughly 12,000 are international alumni.

ANU has 15 coordinators outside Australia who volunteer to plan events and provide outreach for ANU in their home country. Since ANU wants to continue to cultivate these coordinators and identify more international alumni for their database, events are currently free. ANU is banking on this strategy of attracting the greatest number of alumni with complementary events around the world.

ANU does not have chapters, officers or formal groups. "We don't do the formal thing," explains Keller Smith, "because we live in a postmodern world and the world is littered with alumni chapters which don't meet. There is a lot of alumni fatigue out there. There is a lot of administration around chapters. In my experience, we would have these chapter committees of people spending all the time busy with the minutiae of the organization."

Keller Smith's point fits for her side of the world. "I'm disillusioned about the chapter alumni network for ANU [vs. the U.S. model]. The U.S. alumni may feel they owe the university something."

What *has* worked well for ANU is their coordinator network and the staff's ability to coordinate regional visits with traveling faculty members. Typically, an alumni event involving the faculty will also provide an update on a strategic academic area for ANU.

There is one exception for ANU: an alumni chapter in Japan sponsors many events and is governed by elected officers—an approach preferred by alumni in that more formal society. Rather than require uniformity across alumni circles, however, ANU has let its regional alumni influence the engagement strategy. "We are showing we're culturally flexible," adds Keller Smith.

University of Auckland

Amanda Lyne is the manager of alumni relations at the University of Auckland (UofA) and spent three years working under ANU's Christine Keller Smith, when she was at the New Zealand institution. Many of the university's advancement staff members work with international alumni. As Lyne explains, "We only have two dedicated advancement staff based in the U.K./U.S. whose sole responsibility is international alumni. All other alumni/fundraising staff are based in Auckland and are involved to a greater or lesser degree with international as well as local and regional alumni. The director of external relations, myself and the events manager have the most direct contact with international alumni, primarily through events and communications. My alumni relations administrator is responsible for keeping in touch with international volunteer alumni coordinators and helping them to run informal events. The external relations events team (comprising three full-time staff) works with me on organizing formal events for international alumni throughout the year." [15]

UofA, founded in 1883, has seven campuses across the country. Total enrollment as of 2009 is 38,551, with 28,026 undergraduate students and 10,525 postgraduates. Of the approximately 137,399 alumni in the UofA database, 103,603, or 75 percent, are addressable; 13,000, or 9.5 percent, represent international alumni from 129 countries. "The international number is lower than what we expect. Many alumni go abroad right after graduation but come back after five to seven years to raise a family. Therefore, the number may be skewed," adds Lyne. (Lyne's team focuses on alumni from the undergraduate program; UofA's graduate schools have their own alumni programs.)

As in Australia, government funding in New Zealand is decreasing each year, and the universities are being asked to cap their fees. UofA has successfully garnered funds for research from outside sources, for example with the help of a university-owned company called "uniservices," which funds large commercialized research projects. But the university is still looking to advancement to help make up any shortfall.

One mechanism is to build relationships with alumni through events which serve the interest and needs of a range of alumni from recent graduates to retirees. "We are still very young here," Lyne says about their programming history. "We have a slightly different market, so some things working in the U.S. won't work here. We've had a process of warming up alumni with a lot of events. We've only been seriously engaging with alumni for the last 15 years."

One of the major programs for the university community and alumni, both local and abroad, is the Distinguished Alumni Award. The university honors five alumni each year and presents a Young Alumni Award annually as well. For the event, Lyne says, "We have the dinner and then on the next day we have a speaker day on campus and ask our award honorees to speak for 45 minutes each. We open this up to students and to the community. We record the presentations and have it available to international chapters."

Lyne's department also draws on distinguished alumni for international programming. In 2009, for example, Professor Ngaire Woods (on the faculty and also a graduate of UofA), spoke in London on global economic governance. A resident of London, Woods was also an adviser to then British Prime Minister Gordon Brown. The UofA's London alumni were able to participate in this "exported" awards program flexibly designed to meet the needs of the local recipient.

Auckland's 28 volunteer alumni coordinator networks are the key sources of contact between the institution and the alumni. UofA's research with these coordinators shows that alumni want shorter programs and more networking opportunities. Overall, younger alumni are attending events, and an indicator as to why may be that more recent graduates completed surveys indicating greater satisfaction with their student experience as well as stronger connections to faculty.

Staff members work with the volunteers to plan simple happy hour events and provide programming stipends for food. Lyne says that the university is also very interested in recruiting younger alumni. "We have an opportunity to try different

> ## TIP
>
> - Distinguished Alumni awards cultivate established international alumni. Recipients are invited back to the campus, are featured speakers, and interact with community.
>
> - Strategically market professional development services to alumni through a designated section within an alumni magazine.

events and train a more mobile group of alumni to be spokespersons for the university. They are connected with social networks as well.

"The challenge for us is that we're at the stage that we need to decide if we are going to have a more formal club structure," continues Lyne. "I've held back from this because we have a local alumni association, and working with them has proven very difficult due to a decline of local volunteers. We don't want to have something going on in perpetuity." Lyne and her staff are looking for other types of models.

Lyne also notes that recent research undertaken for the alumni association will help Auckland plan programs and engage more alumni. An online survey in the fall of 2008 asked 46,000 alumni (those with "good" email addresses) what benefits they desire from their alma mater. Lyne points out that this direct approach is driven by necessity. "Because many of our alumni had low participation patterns as students, it translates over to their alumni life. We are at a point that we must engage them and ask them what they want to see from their university," she adds.

Lyne's team has now broken down the alumni database into five segments: Students as Future Alumni, Young Alumni, Middle-Aged Alumni, Older Alumni and Golden Alumni. The staff is looking at how to cater to each segment with events, communications, benefits and services.

More alumni are making sure they are in touch with the university and vice versa. Before 2004, the alumni magazine was mailed only to alumni association members: 3,000 of the 90,000 alumni, or just 3 percent. Since 2004, all alumni receive the magazine, which has been repositioned to bring different types of stories and to present an array of services to the alumni readership. "Younger alumni are more interested in jobs, events and new courses. We have responded by incorporating a regular Careers Section in our alumni magazine to provide more professional development to our graduates," states Lyne. This is a direct response to a 2008 research report for the alumni association that found that Auckland needed to improve its marketing of alumni benefits and services.

Lyne is optimistic that international alumni relations outreach will continue to be a priority in the near future. Since 2005, Lyne and her team have been working under a vice chancellor who "gets" what they are trying to achieve. "The senior leader and his team know it is much more than fundraising, that the graduates build the reputation of the university," which is known for medicine, bioengineering and marine biology, Lyne says. She and her staff coordinate visits to major international cities every one to two years with the vice chancellor. "This has produced tremendous good will," she adds. "He has a vision that we are a world-class university."

For Lyne and her staff, today's focus is on the undergraduate experience. Even though communication tools will be important to sustain and develop with the volunteer coordinator network abroad, tools alone "don't create relationships, … which is why we need to build a relationship with students before they graduate and communicate the value of staying in touch."

University of Michigan

Steve Grafton, president and CEO of the Alumni Association of the University of Michigan, has been building an international alumni relations program since 1994. Upon his arrival he inherited a tradition of strong alumni connections between the university and its Asian alumni. The first Asian students arrived from China in the 1860s and 1870s and have brought their heritage to Michigan.

Therefore, an international alumni relations program at Michigan is part of the Michigan fabric. With 460,000 alumni, the association's challenge is creating sustainable programs across a large and decentralized institution. Grafton's goals include finding efficiencies within traditional processes such as mailing magazines and materials to alumni chapters.

Grafton and his staff also remain responsive and available to alumni overseas. "We don't need a club in Ann Arbor. They breathe Michigan every day. The farther away you get, however, the more interest [from alumni] in connecting."[16] Today, Michigan stands ready to respond to this interest.

Grafton provides the recent history: "In the early 1990s, Michigan's president went to China and met with alumni. He promised we would return. There was a 10-year delay. The last time Michigan returned was in 2005. Our alumni saw this as a 10-year 'broken promise.'" What Grafton described is more of a fits-and-starts approach for the international alumni relations program.

In 2005, the approach changed. President Mary Sue Coleman went to Beijing and Shanghai to solidify university partnerships. Alumni Association receptions in each city were planned, and alumni responded with waves of excitement and interest. Grafton's office was represented on this trip by another Michigan colleague who, while in China, pledged that the university alumni association would be back in 2006. They kept that promise: Grafton has returned every year since 2006.

Grafton's focus on China represents a high-level effort to build Michigan's relationships in China. He understands the importance of continuity and commitment. "Culturally, it is a lot more serious to *not* keep your word!" emphasizes Grafton.

TIP

- "Talk the talk and walk the walk." Keep your word and maintain consistency in approach.

- Think of the four pillars of engagement (academics, admissions, alumni and development) when developing international alumni relations.

- International groups should not be held to the same expectations as the most active domestic clubs.

He continues, "Alumni know we're committed. Each time we travel, we take a senior university officer and dean with us on the trip. The deans of the engineering school and the business school are now developing their own international alumni efforts." The deans are planning interim meetings on a more regular schedule in an effort to build on their development activities. Michigan's delegation always includes prominent faculty, well-known to the Michigan community in China.

For the Michigan alumni association team, Jo Rumsey is truly the "go-to" person on international alumni relations issues. Rumsey, who is the association's director of international relations, makes a separate trip to the cities that Grafton visits each year and sets up meetings and events with local clubs. Twenty thousand, or 4 percent of the 500,000 Michigan alumni, live outside the United States. Over 45 international University of Michigan contacts volunteer for their regions.

Prior to 2005, Michigan attempted to sustain a larger, more integrated and strategic effort for alumni relations across all schools, but no one was willing to devote the necessary resources to sustain this larger effort. Offices also felt the university lacked a commitment from the top. In 2005 this changed when President Coleman formed a task force on international alumni relations to assess how and why offices across Michigan (from the business school, to international research centers, to the alumni association) worked with their international constituents. The task force analyzed efforts from 2005 through 2010 and then detailed what the alumni association needs in order to successfully partner with the university in the coming years. Coleman's commitment to keeping international alumni relations at the top of her agenda affirms Rumsey's work and is a clear signal to alumni abroad that Michigan is making investments in their relationships with the university.

Rumsey also believes Michigan is becoming more articulate with its international messaging. She explains, "This president intends to have a legacy of an international alumni relations presence. We are now identifying the large chunks [of alumni overseas]. We can now compound the research ties, business relationships, academic partnerships together; all these pieces can have a critical mass to make a difference in the ways alumni are involved with the university.[17] Rumsey argues that Michigan's critical mass of alumni, a recruitment pool, some expression of alumni interest, a strong academic lead and, in turn, development opportunities are essential to maintaining a strong international alumni relations program. It is these four pillars of engagement (academic, admissions, alumni and development; see figure 1.1) that form a solid foundation upon which Michigan is building.

The organizational model for Michigan's international chapters is much more informal than for its domestic chartered clubs. Rather than require international regions to officially register with the Michigan alumni association, Rumsey tries to identify a nucleus of people in each region who are invested in the university and are interested in each other as volunteers for the university. She identifies tasks that have to be done for Michigan (such as hosting faculty visits) and matches volunteers to appropriate tasks. This approach is working well for Rumsey and her 30 Michigan international contacts around the world.

Rumsey believes that the international groups should not be held up to the same expectations as their most active domestic clubs. "We need to look differently about what we expect," she adds. "There are three main considerations: communications, building sustainable networks, and having consistent visibility each year."

What will Michigan's strategy look like for its 20,000 international alumni over the next five years? Rumsey has completed an analysis of the alumni association's outreach from 2005 through 2010 and has identified steps the association should take to partner with the university's efforts to build a purposeful international alumni program from 2010 through 2015. As the association thinks about what it will take for its work in Asia to develop over time, Rumsey also wants to be sure that her contacts feel empowered to propose program ideas and share their ideas on staying involved with Michigan. "I've developed wonderful relationships and, now, I feel as if I'm going to disappoint them," Rumsey says.

Rumsey plans to use Michigan's good work in Asia as a model for other regions that are prospective "hot spots" for the university. "Wherever we go in the world, it will be determined by strong academic, alumni, admissions and development opportunities," she says.

In the future, Michigan may look to develop alumni communities in Africa if the number of alumni becomes significant; likewise, there may be more alumni outreach in Europe if the number of applicants from that region increases. Whatever lies ahead for international programs, Rumsey and the staff have a great alumni reputation to uphold. "The thing that has astounded me is that everywhere around the world, it's the same Michigan experience: same songs, a love of football, an immediate shared experience." Rumsey says that she and the staff can build great programs on this solid base.

University of Chicago

Established in 1892, the University of Chicago has five campuses worldwide. Two are located in Chicago, and its Booth School of Business has campuses in Singapore, Paris and London. Total enrollment each year is approximately 14,600, with 4,825 enrolled as undergraduate students. Of their 183,000 alumni, 45,000 (or close to 25 percent) reside in 174 countries outside the United States. The University of Chicago has a large advancement staff, and some are located in other cities such as London. Stephanie Veit, director, international alumni relations, and Ryann Olson are members of the university's Network Team.[18] Both women work full-time with the alumni groups in areas outside the United States. Veit, who started working at Chicago in

2007, focuses on Europe, Africa, the Middle East, and the Asia-Pacific region. In 2008, she recruited Olson to work with alumni in Central and South America.

"Until 2007 the University of Chicago was not paying attention to international alumni the way the Booth School of Business was," explains Veit.[19] To go from "not doing much" to an active network at the beginning of 2007, the University of Chicago's central alumni relations and development reached out to alumni around the world to let them know the university wanted to support international students on campus and wanted the international alumni to understand that they are part of the students' current and future network of support. According to Veit, the international alumni were honored to be asked. "We've ignored this group of alumni for so long. For me, it's been a straightforward approach: making amends and now understanding their needs," Veit says.

Veit and her colleagues worked hard at their plan. The staff started with a list of 30 contacts around the world. By 2009, the number of alumni clubs had grown from 20 to 33. Ongoing communications between the university and the clubs is sometimes a challenge. "Not all of them are good at telling us what they are doing and what's worked well," Veit adds. Communication is a two-way street, and Veit knows that it's also important for her to be informed about opportunities to showcase the university talent on the road. "We try to know which faculty are traveling abroad, and we're trying to convince the leadership above us that they need to travel internationally.

"Our international alumni efforts have to be volunteer led," Veit asserts. "The alumni know their country and the dynamics in each region so much better than we do." The staff is focused on supporting the clubs so they are sustainable. "We're asking the volunteers to program for monthly happy hours (in some cases with other schools) and encouraging them to recruit local VIP alumni for a distinguished speaker series." The staff is encouraging as many locally driven events as possible to economize costs in what the university is seeing as a growing area for alumni programming. Even when the staff brings a faculty member to meet with international alumni, Veit asks the local volunteers about ways to minimize the out-of-pocket costs (such as catering) which, when added to fixed travel costs for faculty and staff, can make an event very expensive.

> ### TIP
>
> - Recruit new interest and involvement from international alumni by stressing their impact on the international student experience on and off campus.
>
> - Encourage locally driven events to economize costs.
>
> - An international parents' association unifies support for university as a whole.
>
> - Strategize to have strong alumni communities in the regions where the university has developed academic commitments.

The "Chicago Salon" is an example of a new brand of events for the international clubs. These take place in the homes of alumni (thereby minimizing costs) and are intended to provide a comprehensive update on the state of the university. Not all regions can call the event a "salon." In Japan, for example, this would conjure up a more intimate connotation than the university wants.

The University of Chicago has developed an international alumni handbook. "Many of our peer institutions have similar information: bylaws, event planning tips, liability guidelines," explained Olson. "We're really hoping the handbook is helpful to encourage alumni to send data back to us. We're asking clubs to submit a brief annual report to us once a year. It will be found online and be easy to use."

The university also offers training for its volunteers. In 2007, Veit organized an international forum in London, and all club leaders from around the world were invited. The next forum, which was to be held in Hong Kong in April 2009, had to be postponed because of the economic crisis taking place then. "We will plan future events like this," promises Veit. And although the Hong Kong forum didn't take place, the university did hold a volunteer caucus in Chicago in October 2009. Alumni volunteers paid their own travel expenses, but the university covered meals and meeting costs. During the caucus, presentations offered a review of club guidelines, and a session focused on international best practices. Attendees included five volunteers from India, Mexico, Paris and Hong Kong. Caucus participants received program material on a USB drive, and the university put the materials online for all volunteers to access.

With their initial hands-on approach, much like that of Stanford's alumni association, the University of Chicago aspires to build international alumni clubs beyond the 33 existing today. Olson continues, "Most of our volunteers with whom I work are brand new clubs for us. We're focusing on developing groups in Argentina, Chile, Brazil, and Mexico."

Currently, parents are invited to all international club events. Another new step to complement the inclusive nature of Chicago's outreach is the formation of a new shared interest group for international parents. This is managed by the university's parents program and is an opportunity to yield broader support for the university overseas.

Veit and the rest of the staff acknowledge that the international alumni relations strategy is coming from their president. "It defines our roles, and we have a lot of autonomy in doing what we do," confirms Veit. The overall strategy is to have strong alumni communities where the university has developed academic commitments in several regions:

1. **Southeast Asia and in China.** The university has announced the opening of a campus in Beijing, and the Booth School of Business has a campus in Singapore. Veit spent much of 2008 and 2009 in China building a community in advance of the university opening up the campus. Japan still ranks as the largest Asian alumni region for the university.

2. **India.** Many Indian students apply to the Booth School of Business and other graduate programs.

3. **South America.** Although the university recognizes Brazil as its hub in this region, "we are very strong in Chile and Argentina" as well, says Veit. "For example, in Chile, many of our science faculty members are working with the Chilean observatories such as the Magellan Telescope at Las Campanas Observatory. We traveled there for the first time in June 2009, and we were amazed with the warm reception we received."

But some alumni were hesitant, she adds. This new level of university support and alumni association interest in their region was altogether new.

The institution is well on its way to changing perceptions. With the right combination of leadership and resources, the University of Chicago's efforts to build relationships overseas with its alumni, parents, and friends will ultimately turn a more skeptical alumni observer into a well-informed advocate.

Business Schools

UCLA Anderson School of Management

UCLA Anderson School of Management welcomed a new dean, Judy Olian, on January 1, 2006. Under new leadership, the school is executing a comprehensive strategic plan to broaden its global presence and partnerships. Olian has given an international direction to the school and hired key professionals to help facilitate a united approach to her goals.

Bob Pettit, former executive director of alumni relations and now executive director, UCLA-UAI Global Executive MBA Program, was one of Olian's early hires. In his first year, Pettit hired Mary Fleshood, alumni relations manager, to work with a new Anderson alumni board of directors whose members support student and alumni efforts to secure management and industry positions. The strategic plan for Anderson called upon a change in resources. Soon, Fleshood's position expanded to include work with international alumni.

"The value proposition for our business schools is to be a vital partner in the success of the personal growth of our alumni," says Pettit. "Our goals are to speak about alumni relations early and often. Facebook groups for the incoming students (e.g., UCLA Anderson MBA Class of 2011) are managed by the alumni relations staff."[20]

Some changes in brand identity have also occurred. What was once called UCLA Anderson Alumni is now the UCLA Anderson Alumni Network. The emphasis is to convey the message of the network.

UCLA increased its investment in Anderson's alumni program as the school reached its 75th anniversary in 2010. The school does not have a separate dues-paying association; rather, the alumni relations program is included in the school budget.

In alignment with domestic alumni chapters, Fleshood has been formalizing the international chapters with emphasis on Asia, including greater China and India. Both domestic and international chapters have organizational guidelines in their bylaws. These guidelines help maintain consistency across chapters and allow for greater alumni involvement over time. Before the guidelines were in place, for example, an active volunteer in Spain with ambitions to serve Anderson in greater ways was concerned that one person (who held a two-year term) was the only alumni in a leadership position for the country. To provide an opportunity for more alumni to become active, the guidelines now suggest that each chapter's leadership team be made up of a president, a vice president of events and a treasurer. A structured election process allows for additional opportunities for alumni recognition. In Spain, the outgoing president was lauded as an outstanding volunteer of the year. In addition, the Anderson Spain chapter is recognized under Spanish law, enabling the alumni group to hold membership in the country's business school alliance. Anderson's success, therefore, is contingent on strong leaders and chapter management.

> **TIP**
>
> - Convey the value of the community by renaming alumni association a "network."
> - Both domestic and international chapters have organizational guidelines in their bylaws.
> - Guidelines help maintain consistency across chapters and allow for greater alumni involvement over time.
> - Ideal age for a business school alumni chapter president is 10 to 15 years out (as opposed to a recent alumnus).
> - A best practice is the regularly scheduled conference calls with international leaders and their board members.

Pettit and his team began their efforts in Latin America in 2007. They focused on Mexico and coordinated a trip with their dean. In less than two months, the alumni office had prepared a call for nominations, and in February 2008 the alumni elected a new president for a three-year term. By May 2008, Pettit and the team went to Argentina to facilitate the same process.

The strategy for starting up a chapter is to capitalize on the momentum generated by the dean's trip abroad. After a chapter is established, Anderson asks it to sponsor a minimum of four events a year, one of which should be a social to welcome new alumni to the various cities and countries during Anderson Worldwide Welcome Week. All events are intended to be casual and to break even financially.

Anderson is collaborative across the UCLA community. International alumni also volunteer as admissions representatives. "We play it both ways," stated Pettit. "Some of our alumni are active in UCLA chapters and some are active for admissions."

One of Anderson's best practices is the regularly scheduled conference calls with Latin American alumni leaders and their board members. In the summer, admissions focuses on the conference call agenda as the admissions staff review their fall recruitment calendar with interested alumni. The admissions staff and chapter leaders are introduced to each other, and the recruiters share their travel schedules with chapter board members.

Chapter members not only provide local support for the recruiters who may be new to their regions but also give character references for candidates they meet during the application process.

INSEAD (Institut Européen d'Administration des Affaires)

INSEAD—"The business school for the world"—was founded in 1957 by Georges Doriot, a Harvard graduate whose dream was to create a business school in Europe that was international, independent and close to business. INSEAD is a school with European roots and an international focus. Besides campuses in Europe, Asia and the Middle East, INSEAD has a center in Israel and an office in New York, thereby creating a presence on several continents.

The school's curriculum is also unique. It offers a 10-month MBA program, and MBA and PhD students have the opportunity to study in Fontainebleau and/or Singapore. INSEAD also has an alliance with the Wharton School of Business, affording students an opportunity to study in the United States. For this program, however, Wharton alumni are not considered INSEAD alumni and vice versa. Additional programs at INSEAD include Executive Education and the Global Executive MBA, including a partnership with Tsinghua University in China and a third campus in Abu Dhabi.

INSEAD's focus has been international from the start. "The nature of who we are and what we are includes international alumni relations. We're spread out and diverse—almost everybody is from somewhere else," says Marisa Cooke, director of alumni affairs and the INSEAD Alumni Fund.[21]

INSEAD takes both a centralized and decentralized approach to alumni organizations. The school's 40,000 alumni live in more than 160 countries; it has 43 national alumni associations in 46 countries (with Australia and New Zealand sharing one association). In addition, it maintains 13 country contacts in countries that do not have enough of an alumni base or volunteer network to yet warrant having a full-fledged association. The INSEAD Alumni Association (IAA) is the umbrella organization over the country contacts and the national alumni associations. The IAA president and six alumni form the executive committee, or the Ex-Co. Each member of the Ex-Co is responsible for a particular world region and has contact with each association president within that region.

Cooke and Craig McKenna, associate director of alumni relations and services, and their staff work closely with the Ex-Co. Meetings for the professional staff and the Ex-Co are held at least four times a year and biannual meetings, called the IAA General Assemblies, bring the 43 national alumni associations together with the Ex-Co and the school. One meeting each year is held on the main campus in France; the other meeting is held offsite. Highly organized, the meetings allow for regional reports, and participants vote on matters of policy, strategy and budget. In the interim, the staff works with the Ex-Co to follow up on action items. The General Assembly in the spring is usually combined with INSEAD's leadership summit weekend on campus. In the fall of each year, the IAA General Assembly is usually hosted by one of the national associations and incorporates a local high-profile event. "On campus, we work with the MBA Department to spread the message about our alumni network," Cooke says. "We work with the Executive Education department to do the same thing." Additionally, the alumni staff members work with the career services office, which has a dedicated alumni career services person on staff. The alumni office also facilitates faculty travel to regional alumni events throughout the year.

The net product of INSEAD's efforts is internally very centralized and professional, yet the staff strives to maintain a balance between having too much control and not enough. The 43 associations have websites and can send out emails based on their own schedule. Each year, McKenna's team trains association "administrators" to use the different resources, including online tools and websites. For example, the staff and volunteer leaders work together to ensure consistent branding across the national alumni associations. Although the associations are independent when it comes to sending communications to their network, INSEAD provides support for managing email traffic, data and bounce-backs.

To further promote the INSEAD alumni brand during the institution's 50th anniversary year, the school produced a downloadable toolkit, including banners, letterhead and websites for each of the 43 alumni associations. Web-based material also included the school's logo and an icon of IAA's salamander symbol.

General Assemblies include much time for networking and best-practice workshops. McKenna explains: "We spend a lot of time on INSEAD Connect [the

> ## TIP
>
> - An umbrella organization above country contacts and the national alumni associations can serve as the executive body for all alumni. Professional staff liaise with this executive body to set policy and make major decisions.
>
> - The General Assembly held twice a year is the official business meeting for the alumni association.
>
> - Hold one major alumni association meeting in another region of the world in coordination with a major event.
>
> - Train association "administrators" to use the different communications including online tools and websites.
>
> - Online community portal includes a resource center of best practices from and for associations.

school's online community portal] on a macro level. We get into details with the administrators of each association and ask presidents to participate in best practice workshops." More experienced leaders share their planning steps and serve as peer resources to presidents of newer, smaller associations.

IESE (Instituto de Estudios Superiores de La Empresa)

IESE is the business school of the University of Navarra in Spain. The school was founded in 1958. Six years later, the school, in collaboration with Harvard University, launched its first MBA program. It has campuses in Madrid and Barcelona and additional facilities in Munich, New York and Sao Paolo.

A graduate school, it has two main degree programs: a full-time, two-year MBA program that enrolls 200 students per year, and an executive education series, with a variety of programs offered in Europe, the United States and China.

More educational opportunities are offered outside Spain than within its borders, but the school seeks to bring more international students to its Madrid and Barcelona campuses. As Wim den Tuinder, associate director of the alumni division, explains, "Internationalization is building gradually over time. Our MBA is the program where we see a higher increase in students from abroad. Now more than 80 percent of our participants come from outside of Spain. Our Executive MBA has evolved to bring in others from outside of Spain as well, and our programs abroad attract international students." [22]

Den Tuinder manages the activity for IESE alumni outside Spain. Of the approximately 34,500 alumni, about 20 percent live and work abroad. This number is increasing each year. IESE alumni are organized through alumni chapters, and den Tuinder's team applies structure to the overall network of 30 alumni chapters. Twenty-two chapters are international, and each is governed by a chapter board made up of five to 10 alumni who voluntarily work with the office and lead the plan of activity from year to year.

Chapters developed over time, says den Tuinder. "From 2000, there were 11 chapters outside of Spain. In nine years it has doubled, and there are new chapters developing all over the place. There are about 10 chapters in Europe, including Russia, two chapters in North America, and others in Latin America and Asia." IESE is developing more chapters in major metropolitan areas. "For the moment, we have no chapters in the Middle East and Africa, but this will probably change in the next two years as our alumni are increasingly widespread," says den Tuinder.

IESE relies on membership dues to fund alumni outreach and activities. Any graduate may become a member of the IESE Alumni Association, and alumni have an option to become paying members, a notion gaining popularity among all alumni desiring preferred access to professional development programs and career coaching. Today, 43 percent of alumni pay dues each year. The annual dues fee differs for Spanish residents (€410) and nonresidents of Spain (less than €200), and the nearly 100 percent markup is due to the greater number of continuing education sessions offered to alumni inside Spain. Den Tuinder expects this to change. "The fees we charge outside of Spain will go up as services are increased, and we might charge fees on a specific-service basis. The story here is that rather than pay for a menu of services we also insist that, apart from services and activities, we expect members to financially and personally contribute to growing a strong network and community." IESE knows this is a challenging idea to support, but the institution is confident that the message will spread and alumni will want to be part of something bigger than their regional chapters.

IESE's alumni association was founded with the first graduating class in 1959. Members of this inaugural class asked for ways they could continue their education and stay in touch with the school.

"For us on a particular international level this is a strong formula for promoting IESE in other places around the world," says den Tuinder. "We are delivering on what the alumni want when we were founded in 1958. The whole idea of having access to continuing learning is a distinct element. It is the number one reason our alumni association exists." IESE believes this distinction sets the school apart from other international business schools. Networking aside, the creation of continuing education opportunities remains a strategic priority.

Having the right staff in place is also strategic. Den Tuinder's role since his arrival in 2005 has been international chapter development. Because of the strong IESE heritage in Spain, the school's strategic plan included using international alumni chapters to promote the school abroad. "The interesting thing was that this was also the number one thing to help satisfy our international alumni," he adds. "All of the events we plan promote the school and its different programs. We work together with teams of international executive education so we can sell the program. We also have an enormous opportunity to grow," says den Tuinder.

TIP

- Creation of continuing education opportunities remains a strategic priority. Faculty presenters are key to programs.
- A highly structured governance provides better coordination and accountability.
- Major global reunions occur once a year in different regions. Strive to alternate locations in a sequential way as to come back to the home campus every three years.
- Provide a live Internet transmission of a major reunion event for alumni around the world.
- Consider co-sponsoring global reunions with other business schools to expand resources and reach to the international business community.

IESE's alumni association is now a model for other departments and programs on campus. In the past, internal collaboration between functional areas had always been more territorial, but today programs are asking about the association's model for alumni infrastructure. Prospective students are also asking about alumni networks, thus creating a value proposition worthy of marketing among admissions officers. Alumni also participate in MBA fairs, open houses and interview days around the world. These events include presentations by professors in a simulated classroom environment. Alumni assist by answering questions about the schools and sharing their own experiences as students and, now, professionals. The admissions office will coordinate the contact with alumni around the world in efforts of organizing these annual events.

These are new ways of operating, says den Tuinder. "When we proactively incorporate what we do with alumni, more often than not it is a real eye opener." Since the alumni association is not a separate entity from the school, the staff manages the day-to-day operations and has the ability to keep the alumni database a current and active resource for the work of the staff and alumni leaders.

IESE's alumni association is governed by both administration and volunteers. Its executive committee is chaired by the dean of the school and includes both alumni association staff and local alumni. This body meets every other month.

At one level underneath the executive committee, there is a governing board of the alumni association that includes the executive committee, all chapter presidents and all class presidents and secretaries elected from each graduating class. The whole structure combines class and regional representations. "The combination of these groups is an enormous help to keep this all together" believes den Tuinder. The board meets once a year and produces a financial report and an annual report that are included in IESE's institutional annual report.

From this governing body hang the chapter boards. The chapters are centralized in their governance and their management to the extent that the alumni office supports all chapters with their event publicity and logistical needs. "We want to brand IESE and make it official, and the key to all of this is that we control and maintain the database," explains den Tuinder.

On a yearly basis IESE and its alumni chapters organize roughly 200 events across the world, and approximately 80 occur outside Spain. The average number of events per chapter ranges from one a month to one a quarter in a given year. The most common types of events include:

- **Continuing education sessions.** Held after office hours, these one-hour programs are delivered by an IESE professor and/or a guest speaker. Faculty involvement is crucial. "To do this regularly we depend on our faculty," says den Tuinder. "We have a committed and understanding faculty who know exactly what the alumni association's strategy is. This is absolutely key." A networking reception follows these sessions, and prospective students are often invited to participate as a way to meet the faculty and the alumni.

- **Global reunions.** Major global reunions occur once a year in different regions. IESE alternates locations between Barcelona and Madrid, and every third year the reunion occurs outside of Spain. The 2006 Global Reunion was held in Munich as the school launched its Executive Education program in Germany; the 2009 Global Reunion took place in New York City as part of the IESE's plan to present itself to the business community in the United States. The 2012 Global Reunion will also coincide with the beginning of a new international academic initiative.

Reunions in Spain typically attract 1,500 alumni and their guests. In order to give alumni around the world a chance to participate in the Barcelona and Madrid reunion programs, IESE provides a live Internet transmission of the event. In the past, another 2,000 alumni have been able to enjoy a virtual connection to the main reunion speakers and the sessions. Former president of Harvard and then-U.S. Treasury Secretary Lawrence Summers spoke at the October 2008 Global Reunion. His speech took place at 8:30 a.m. in Madrid; alumni in the United States stayed connected at 2:30 a.m. to see the session. Even with the nontraditional viewing hours for alumni around the world, the response received from this type of access and inclusion was very positive.

Den Tuinder is optimistic about the future. "Day to day, I see more and more alumni understanding how we're working and what we have to offer. Once they understand this, their enthusiasm increases and more chapters form. The challenge is to ask how to involve them so that we work for each other. It's a delicate balance of having them support the school and having them feel supported."

The staff wants to continue to find ways that make it easy for their international alumni to stay engaged. Technology is one. How IESE develops and incorporates social networks into its database management and chapter outreach is an ongoing initiative. Podcasts, e-conferences, and other web tools are others.

Recent economic realities produced a third type of programming model for the alumni association: career orientation. IESE hosts a job site on its web site and makes available other professional tools, such as career self-assessment modules and résumé tip sheets. This is a young programming area (1.5 FTEs in the alumni association work on career programs), but it is developing quickly with help of the career services department. The tools that this office uses for students are being adapted for alumni. "We are also asking faculty to help in this area by presenting programs in areas of competency development and coaching," states den Tuinder. He believes that this area will be much more developed by 2015.

Finally, IESE sees a potential for collaborating with other schools. One idea is to co-sponsor global alumni reunions with similar schools. Combining resources to sponsor major speakers and networking events abroad can become one smart way of offering joint solutions for alumni seeking greater access to an international business community.

ENDNOTES

1. Harold Brown, director of alumni relations, interview with author, Cambridge, MA, June 9, 2009.

2. Val Iwashita, telephone interview with author, June 2, 2009.

3. "Alumni in Japan Celebrate," *'Iolani School Bulletin* (Spring 2011). *www.iolanibulletin.org/issues/2011/spring/_other_news/alumni_events_activities#Japan.*

4. Information about ISKL from Toni Mullen, telephone interview with author, May 26, 2009, and interview with author, Cape Cod, MA, July 16, 2009.

5. "Planning a Reunion—An Idea Checklist," *community.asij.ac.jp/Page.aspx?pid=436;* Shin Takei, "Class Reunion Organizing Survival Guide" (American School in Japan, 1993), *www.asij.ac.jp/alumni/Class%20Reunion%20Guide.pdf.*

6. Matt Wilce, director of communications and the annual fund, telephone interview with author, June 10, 2009.

7. Andrea Booth, telephone interview with author, June 10, 2009.

8. Debra Price, telephone interview with author, June 10, 2009.

9. Charlotte Armah, telephone interview with author, July 6, 2009.

10. For a sample of the survey, see *www.surveymonkey.com/s.aspx?sm=O9cTSWDclCCrSRcpYKcrbLnH9yIkrTTNbfdfpeEEI08%3d#q1.*

11. Sanjeev Aggarwall, telephone interview with author, July 24–25, 2009.

12. Steve Suda, telephone interview with author, June 22, 2009.

13. Robert M. Moore, "To Market, To Market: Higher Education Refines Its Approach in Canada, the United Kingdom, and Australia," CURRENTS 34 (January 2008): 37, 40.

14. Christine Keller Smith, telephone interview with author, Sept. 2, 2009.

15. Amanda Lyne, email correspondence with author, Nov. 13, 16, 2010.

16. Steve Grafton, telephone interview with author, July 6, 2009.

17. Jo Rumsey, telephone interview with author, July 6, 2009.

18. Since this was written, Olson has become the senior associate, alumni network, at Price Waterhouse Coopers.

19. Stephanie Veit, telephone interview with author, summer, 2009, and interview with author, Chicago, Dec. 14, 2009.

20. Bob Pettit, interview with author, Los Angeles, Aug. 3, 2009.

21. Marisa Cooke, telephone interview with author, Aug. 11, 2009.

22. Wim den Tuinder, telephone interview with author, Oct. 19, 2009.

STUDENT-ALUMNI PROGRAMMING

Independent Schools

United World College of South East Asia

Some schools have discovered the hard way that getting students involved *before* they leave campus is a great way to avoid "losing" alumni. The United World College of South East Asia (UWCSEA) was one of these schools.

Founded in 1971, UWCSEA boasts well over 20,000 alumni; but over the years, it had lost track of most of them. In 2006, the school committed a full-time staff member to set up a comprehensive alumni program as part of its new advancement department, to reconnect with alumni and try to locate some of the "lost" ones.

The staff also knew it would be important to connect with their current students on campus to avoid losing these students in the future. To that end, UWCSEA has begun to promote its alumni relations program to graduating students before they complete their final year, encouraging them to join the alumni online community and/or provide their contact details before they move on. In addition, they have developed a program that provides an opportunity for students to serve on an alumni council. This program encourages students in their last two years of school to become active members on the council. In turn, they receive community service hours, which are a graduation requirement for all UWCSEA students. The students on the council help with the annual reunion planning and organization as well as with the biannual alumni magazine, and they provide assistance to the office with tasks such as conducting surveys about social networking usage in general and, more specifically, among alumni.

TIP

- Involve students with the alumni council: students become volunteers and are trained early about alumni association benefits.

- Invite international alumni to advise students on the college search process.

- Encourage enrollment in an online community before graduation. Highlight benefits of becoming connected for life.

Participation in the alumni council helps students beyond fulfilling graduation requirements. They are introduced to the idea of being part of the alumni community and to the benefits that lie therein. For instance, while assisting with the annual alumni reunion weekend they are able to meet and talk to alumni who are reconnecting with old classmates and friends as well as the college, often after many years. The interaction between these students and the alumni fosters a sense of continuity between these two groups. As mentioned, students in the 12th grade are invited to join the alumni online community, ensuring that UWCSEA has the students' contact information and providing students with access to alumni services. In the past few years more than half of each graduating class has joined the alumni website before or shortly after graduation.

The password-protected alumni website was one of UWCSEA's first steps in its efforts to reclaim its lost alumni and create an alumni community. Graduates of UWCSEA can maintain their own profile page, search for other alums, register for events and more. The site also has a list of names of "lost" alumni, grouped by class year, which has been very successful in locating alumni. Friends or alumni themselves, seeing their names on the list, can click a button that allows them to easily send their location and contact information to the alumni office. The alumni office can then invite them to join the site. The staff also conducted research on other alumni programs and created a menu of online and other services that they monitor and continually work to enhance and expand. Today the alumni program includes a web portal, an electronic newsletter, a biannual alumni magazine, a presence on several major social networking sites, a reunion program and a new student-alumni mentor program.

UWCSEA recently added to its website a mentoring program, which links current senior students with alumni willing to offer advice and/or information about universities and careers. Here, alumni are asked to provide their name, university attended, dates of attendance, field of study, career field and preferred contact information. Current UWCSEA seniors may browse the listings, and when they see one that interests them, they can click to send an email directly to the alumnus. UWCSEA hopes this service will be of great assistance to students when considering their university and career choices, and staff will monitor its usage and usefulness to that end. Through this program, seniors will be given the opportunity to benefit from speaking to UWCSEA alumni who have studied all over the world. The alumni office and the university counselors promote the program.

Phillips Exeter Academy

At Phillips Exeter Academy, the alumni association works closely with the school administration and the students to ensure the continuation of traditions old and new. A pinning ceremony during the Exeter alumni council's fall meeting introduces students to alumni and alumni to students. Considered a "new" tradition, this ceremony, which began in 2005, is the latest extension of one of the most robust, nostalgic alumni legacies in the United States. Exeter realizes a robust 50 percent participation rate with its annual giving program. One of the factors in this success is a commitment to student-alumni interaction.

Exeter offers another point of connection between students and graduates by bringing alumni to campus throughout the school year. For example, two "Fireside Chats" featured alumni who served on the U.S. presidential campaign team for then-candidate Barack Obama and others with expertise in environmental sustainability. The election conversation in particular resonated with young adults and helped forge connections between groups.

Another way in which Exeter alumni and students interact is during reunions, which are held while school is in session. Over the course of four weekends in the spring, Exeter brings back 12 classes, starting with their most recent graduating classes (the 5th/10th reunion classes) and stretching all the way to its 70th reunion class. Each year's 50th Reunion class returns on its own weekend and celebrates with all students. Each 50th Reunion class also shares a special ceremony—and a special connection—with the students who are seniors that year. Each senior class builds its own annual fund, and the amount raised by the students is matched by that year's 50th Reunion class. For example, in 2009, the senior class raised $5,685; with the match of $5,685 from the 50th Reunion class, the total gift was $11,370. However, the money did not stop there. Pride in the first match prompted the Class of '59 to add $25,000 to the class of 2009's 25th Reunion fund. The student effort was recognized by alumni; with growing momentum, alumni recognized their peers by extending their own contributions one step further to establish a fund that will grow over the next 25 years. The senior gift program is 10 years old, but perhaps the type of commitment exhibited by the Class of '59 will become a new tradition for Exeter.

> ## TIP
>
> - Host alumni speaker programs around "hot topics" and current events.
> - Capitalize on the reunion program by developing intergenerational ceremonies and annual fund initiatives.

American School in Japan

With between 6,000 and 7,000 U.S.-based alumni and current students, ASIJ tried to facilitate an ambassador program in 2005 and 2006 that allowed alumni to self-identify as hosts or resources in their cities. The school hoped that these general alumni connections would help with student recruitment and provide local opportunities for alumni to socialize. The effort did not succeed and was hard to manage, since the school does not have alumni chapters in cities outside Japan. Adding to this challenge is the strong, vocal and organized local Tokyo-based alumni association that provides much of the financial and volunteer support for student athletics and awards programs.

Andrea Booth, alumni relations officer, recounts the history of the local chapter and how local alumni felt about regional affiliates. "About four to five years ago, ASIJ looked at having international chapters, and there was some pushback from the local chapter that felt they represented all alumni," Booth explains.[23] Today, ASIJ tries to focus the Tokyo-based local chapter's energies on campus events and committee work. "They wear a unique hat because they have students of their own at ASIJ," adds Booth. These legacy students on campus are a focus for the local alumni. The alumni relations staff has asked parents to sponsor programs such as a travel fund for high school student activities (e.g., Model United Nations, sports teams) with the ongoing goal of having an extra source of financial support to send ASIJ student groups out on the road for these competitions.

> ## TIP
>
> - A local alumni group feels investment in the success of the program. Tap into this local energy and consider other ways of servicing the needs of international alumni.
>
> - Scale is important. Decide on reasonable expectations for programs involving students and alumni abroad. Test the waters, observe and then move on if the program is not sustainable.

For the coming years, ASIJ will focus its efforts on building a communications strategy for engaging alumni of all years around the globe in order to create stronger partnerships between alumni and students. Some programs and services may be overhauled to allow for innovation and efficiency.

International School in Kuala Lumpur

The International School in Kuala Lumpur (ISKL), established in 1965 to serve a primarily diplomatic core of expatriates, is a college-preparatory school offering a rigorous academic program for 1,650 students. The school serves students from more than 60 nations with a concentration from the United States, Japan and Korea, but places a cap of 20 percent on any one nationality.

At ISKL, alumni affairs has organized a program called College Connections. Alumni currently attending colleges and universities around the world volunteer to be resources to prospective students and families from ISKL. Because the program is easy to promote and does not take much time from alumni volunteers, the number of registered connectors is increasing each year. As of 2010, the number of College Connections volunteers was approximately 700. The process is managed by the alumni director, who speaks to the current seniors and emails reminders that this service is available. The "insider" view from a younger ISKL alumnus is that students researching college choices value this program very highly.

Interested seniors received a list of relevant volunteers; then, it's up to the students to connect with the appropriate alumni to ask questions about the universities being considered. A similar program, Career Connections, is also provided to ISKL alumni. When alumni register online for College Connections, they can opt in to their own networking community.

Benenden School

Benenden's Hong Kong alumni base is well-organized, and it shows. During every school holiday, the Hong Kong alumni organize a tea party for Benenden students visiting home. In an ongoing fashion, alumni take an active interest in the students and encourage dialogue with them; students share information about their on-campus experiences, and alumni are generous with college and career advice. The Hong Kong alumni group is different from other Benenden groups: Each member pays annual dues, which helps fund teas and other special events for alumni and students. In August 2009, Benenden Development Director Debra Price traveled to Hong Kong to attend a preview of the latest Harry Potter movie. Alumni rented a private theater, and students new to Benenden were invited as well.

The benefits of involving students in alumni programs on campus and in international alumni programs abroad are evident. Bringing students and alumni together on leadership boards and for reunions and campus programs furthers the opportunities to build relationships across generations. Mentor programs succeed in bridging professional experiences and skills while enabling international groups an opportunity to sponsor seasonal or year-round programs unique to their region. Altogether, increased interaction is positive, for students, alumni and schools alike.

Colleges and Universities

University of Cambridge

The venerable university is 800 years old and ready to change with the times.

"We have not historically worked with current students, but we'd like to do that," says Nathalie Walker, head of alumni relations for the University of Cambridge, about alumni-student programming.[24] Cambridge's alumni program is faced with long-standing operating models, such as the way admissions handles all the interaction with prospective students from application stage through acceptance.

"Cambridge is very different than what it was 30 years ago," Walker continues. "We need a very robust alumni training program to teach students about what Cambridge in the 21st century is about. Having the leadership acknowledge this as well is one step closer to building a model program at the university."

Cambridge's vice chancellor until October 2010, Professor Alison Richard, a 30-year veteran of Yale, arrived at Cambridge in 2003 and immediately prepared for their capital campaign, which was launched publicly in 2005. Richard favored a strong alumni relations program rooted in building relationships and participation to complement the fundraising efforts of the university. The collegiate model of Cambridge (whereby students affiliate with their residential colleges) provides strong foundations for sustaining links with alumni, but the university centrally also has a responsibility to support and engage alumni across the college structure.

> **TIP**
>
> • Choose a good time and city for alumni and students to socialize. Students are the special guests.
> • Alumni groups may charge annual dues to cover the costs of the student-alumni events.

Cambridge is in touch with 185,000 alumni. Twenty-five percent (or 46,250) live outside the U.K., 14,000 live in North America and the remaining reside in other countries. Twenty-seven percent of Cambridge alumni graduated after 1995, and the university has email addresses for about 40 percent of its alumni.

Student enrollment is up at Cambridge. Additionally, the "lost rate" of alumni has decreased over time. Staff are noticing the trend of higher student numbers, better record keeping and the university's desire to reach out to more alumni. This combination of factors, plus a major campaign, provides impetus to student/alumni partnerships.

Cambridge is still a decentralized university. Most undergraduates identify with their own college and their own academic department. There are 31 individual colleges and all alumni are alumni of both a college and the university. Each college sponsors its own alumni activities. Additionally, Cambridge alumni are involved in over 300 groups around the world, some of which are college-specific international alumni groups. The university has its own sister organization in North America called Cambridge in America, or CAm for short. Kathy Lord, director of alumni relations for CAm, liaises with 44 regional groups across the United States. "Without a campus to return to, we try to bring the brilliance of Cambridge to the States," explains Lord.[25] In addition to the scheduled faculty programs, CAm's 800th Anniversary Gala was held in New York City in December 2009.

Walker and her staff believe their work with younger graduates is becoming a best practice. Walker explains, "Relatively few groups make this transition well (as many are led by retired men). Alumni now recognize that they can lead separate sub-groups to make sure that alumni from different generations can be involved." For example, the Land Society—an alumni society of the academic department for Land Economy majors—is a relatively new alumni group. Supporting segmentation within groups is one way to customize an appeal to a new audience.

> ## TIP
>
> - Don't operate as if one model fits all. Respect and support varying models of building community among students and promote the opportunity to form shared interests before graduation.
> - Design programs that bring the campus experience to alumni. Involve students in programs.

University of Toronto in Hong Kong

The largest international alumni body in Hong Kong is the alumni of University of Toronto (U of T). The university has more than 475,000 alumni, and some 10,000 live in Hong Kong. Roughly 10 percent of the 47,000 undergraduate students are international. From 1978 to 1993, the university made regular visits to the city and in 1993 the advancement department asked Krista Slade, a U of T graduate and now director of advancement at Oxford University's Rhodes House, to work part-time with area graduates as a means to build support for the university and its larger philanthropic goals. In 2003, Slade and a larger staff expanded the scope of the office in Hong Kong to incorporate additional primary functions of a regional office. Today, three staff members support functions throughout Asia. Admissions programs are just one of the ways U of T is inviting its international alumni to become involved in helping carry out its strategic plan.

> ## TIP
>
> - With a regional advancement office, recruit, train, and recognize alumni who serve as ambassadors and interviewers for admissions.
> - Invite all members of the regional community to participate in international send-off events.

As part of its strategic efforts in the area of recruitment in Asia-Pacific, U of T has its area alumni serve as spokespersons at admissions fairs. Alumni are also involved in send-off activities. Older alumni provide moral support to parents who may experience their first son or daughter traveling abroad. Recently, U of T counted over 1,000 alumni, parents and new students participating in summer send-off events in 10 major centers across Asia.

The University of Toronto Asia-Pacific advancement office in Hong Kong oversees regular outreach to China, Singapore, Japan, Korea, Taiwan and Southeast Asia. Each staff member at the office is trained to do everything: marketing, communications, development, alumni relations and international recruitment. This cross-training approach is intended to help the staff check off multiple priorities. "I think every advancement officer should go through recruitment training at the school," states Jeremy Woodall, formerly with the U of T Hong Kong office.[26] "We are cultivating the next alumni pool. We talk about the alumni networks in Asia while we are recruiting."

Stanford University

Send-off activities are a tradition at Stanford University. As a way to begin the lifelong relationship between the students and Stanford, the university's alumni association and the clubs around the world sponsor send-offs during August and September. New students are directed to a web page and find a message like this recent one:

> Welcome to Stanford, Class of 2013! As a newly minted Stanford student, you—and your proud parents—are now officially a part of our extended family of Stanford alumni, parents and students. Come celebrate with your local Stanford community at a New Student Send-Off party in your area.

More than 75 clubs around the United States and the world participated in these send-offs in 2009. The Stanford Alumni Association (SAA) sends written guidelines to alumni chapter leaders in the spring, soon after the new undergraduate class is confirmed. With a systematic plan in place, the SAA is able to help volunteers coordinate logistics, publicity and event supplies. The SAA will even subsidize club send-offs for groups that do not charge dues or when reimbursing an individual host.

National University of Singapore

The National University of Singapore (NUS) was founded in 1905 and, over the last 100 years, has built a reputation as a leading educational institution for law, business, medicine, science and engineering. NUS educates about 36,000 students each year. The Office of Alumni Relations was led by Associate Professor Teo Choo Soo from 2001 to 2010. Today the director is Associate Professor Lim Meng Kin.

During his tenure, Teo built a staff of 38 that works with NUS' 200,000 alumni. Ten percent of the alumni live outside Singapore. NUS tries to take advantage of the large number of local graduates by engaging alumni in the support of the institution. In 2009, NUS opened the Alumni House and welcomed all alumni back "home" to campus. The Alumni House complex was part of Teo's central strategy. During a 2009 interview, he said, "We are trying not only to bridge the gap in alumni cultivation which we see in North America, but also to 'leap-frog' into new experiences."[27]

These "newer" opportunities for alumni include getting involved in both local and overseas alumni groups. There are 15 overseas alumni chapters and 45 local alumni groups that are interest based, residence-hall based or faculty based. Even though the majority of NUS alumni are local and can regularly participate in the campus-based alumni group activities, NUS wants its international alumni to feel included in the ongoing academic, co-curricular and residential lives of the faculty and student body. Thus, all alumni are welcomed to learn more about the groups. With almost 7,000 alumni in neighboring Malaysia, for example, that country provides a good opportunity for "more local" engagement on campus.

According to the *Local Alumni Groups Guidebook*, published by the NUS Office of Alumni Relations, the objectives of local alumni groups include:

- Establish and maintain communication, consultation and co-operation between alumni and NUS.
- Strengthen ties among alumni through the group's social and professional activities.
- Provide services to alumni, including professional development programs undertaken in conjunction with the university.
- Engender support for the university from alumni.
- Take part in making NUS a Global Knowledge Enterprise.

Each of the 45 local alumni groups fulfills these objectives by sponsoring activities, publishing papers and journals and offering mentoring programs for current students. For example, the NUS Economics Alumni group sponsors talks and field trips and has an active mentoring program. The Faculty of Law Alumni group participates in law school career fairs. The University Scholars Programme (USP) also has an alumni network. Since 2003, alumni from this academic honors program are deeply involved in the welfare of the program. Some will interview prospective students as part of the USP admissions interview panel and others will take part in USP student retreats.

Teo wanted the alumni program to be inclusive, but how does the office reach out to everyone? "We have an associate director of alumni relations assigned to each faculty's associate directors. We share information, partner with educational programs, and are building a strong rapport. The faculty knows of our work with alumni and can speak about this (outreach) with the student body," says Teo.

The NUS Volunteer Action Alumni Association has also been promoting volunteerism and philanthropy among NUS alumni since 2003. One of its primary objectives is to promote closer links between the alumni and NUS student volunteer host organizations. Another group, the NUS Alumni Photographic Society, lends support and advice to the campus-based Photographic Society of NUS and is involved in an annual photographic exhibit.

Finally, some of the more established alumni groups are linked to the residential experience. Simply put, these groups promote interaction with current residents and the alumni of the hall to encourage community among a large network and to support the activities and overall welfare of the hall.

NUS' quick work in organizing the local groups is helping the university catch up to other institutional peers. "We cultivate alumni as soon as they arrive as students," adds Teo. "In the traditional Asian university, we didn't pay attention to students. We are working closely to make sure the student experience is a good one."

> **TIP**
>
> • Organize and support alumni groups based on academic major, shared interest and residential experience.
>
> • Early cultivation of the student body is achieved by having active alumni involved in each of the three types of alumni groups: interest based, residence-hall based or faculty based.

University of Navarra in Pamplona

The alumni association at the University of Navarra in Pamplona has begun a successful campaign to recruit first-year students as well as graduating seniors for their alumni association. Although their example does not directly involve international alumni with their students, it is a direct appeal to their "alumni in training."

The university was founded in 1952. Its main campus is in Pamplona, but it also has campuses in San Sebastian, Barcelona and Madrid. Of their 13,197 enrolled students, 8,850 are undergraduates and the rest are enrolled in special studies, master's and doctoral programs. There are 96,605 addressable alumni; of that number, 14,542 reside outside of Spain in more than 100 countries. Navarra has alumni chapters in Spain and in other countries. Jose Luis de Cea, assistant director of the alumni office, explains that "about 7 percent of our undergraduate students come from abroad; and for graduate (students), the percentage is higher, so the average is 12 percent."[28]

De Cea and his staff have made a commitment to testing a new program to engage their students. "Our alumni association is very focused on our students so that we increase members. They have to opt in and pay a fee to become a member." Their strategy is about building a relationship with the new students from Day 1. In

August, the alumni association sends a welcome letter to new students and invites students to meet members of the staff during opening week to learn more about becoming members of the alumni association.

Staff members also leave flyers on tables around campus, advertising the services and benefits of a student alumni association membership. Membership is €10 a year. The association charges a membership fee, says de Cea, because "we want them to … see the value [in membership], and they have to [want to] renew each year." Benefits include discounts at assorted businesses, from ski resorts to copying services to driving lessons. "We also have discounts in the courses offered for students such as cooking and photography." Navarra alumni teach these courses and are encouraged to interact with the students on campus as well in the classroom.

This association's first-time membership campaign in 2008–2009 produced remarkable results: 90 percent of students became members within the first week. How did they do it? "On the first day we left flyers and set up an area to take pictures of all the classes and interview them about their hobbies," de Cea explains. "We get their email addresses and the alumni association creates the yearbook. In the process of creating yearbooks we tell them about the alumni association and the benefits for students and alumni."

Promoting the alumni association is completed throughout the first year, and first-year students who are association members receive yearbooks for no extra fee (non-members pay €5). The university does not publish a yearbook, a tradition seen in other countries. De Cea knows this is a good opportunity. "We are always looking for things the students will like that the university does not provide. We are investing in them!" For the 10 dues per student, the alumni association is paying for the yearbook and flyers. It has become a break-even marketing campaign that Navarra is banking on for the future. "We'll see what happens after they leave the university in four years," says de Cea.

Another similar service provided by the alumni association is the production of an *Orla,* an academic poster that includes pictures of all the students and their senior-year teachers. According to de Cea, many professionals in Spain have this poster in their offices, and it is a point of pride for graduates. "We now add the first-year photo with the last year and mix in their other photos for remembering. This is a service we offer for free. We create a downloadable PDF of the poster."

TIP

- Promote alumni association membership to first-year students.

- Determine levels of services for students not already met by the university.

- Charge nominal dues each year and showcase how services and discounts received are far greater than the cost of the dues.

- Create a class poster as a senior gift to build community, nostalgia and pride.

The University of Navarra is off to an active start with both new and soon-to-be-graduating students. These recent programs have coincided with a young international alumni relations program.

"Internationalization of the university has been very recent" says de Cea, "but for the last 10 years, the international alumni are the most loyal. If you have to travel to get involved, the more loyal you are. Leaving your home to go to University de Navarra means you are committed." With attractive programs for new students, community-building products such as the *Orla* for seniors and now interest from all alumni, local or not, Navarra has a strong combination upon which to build over the coming decade.

Tufts University

At Tufts, and at many universities with a high percentage of international students, international relations is the most popular major. The university shares a campus with its Fletcher School of Law and Diplomacy, affording students an opportunity to take classes at the graduate school and participate in a variety of regularly scheduled symposia and speaker programs featuring international leaders and intellectuals from around the world.

Another unique program at Tufts, the Institute of Global Leadership (IGL), offers students an extraordinary opportunity to "live and learn in the field" with scholars, students and alumni in other parts of the world. In its 27th year, the IGL has graduated 2,500 students and boasts an alumni group of the same size. They are an intimate community. Most students remain involved with IGL for three years, studying photojournalism, negotiation, nongovernmental organizational management and more throughout their academic years, holiday and summer breaks. The IGL alumni are among the program's most ardent supporters, both financially and organizationally serving as student hosts and advisers to students overseas.

> **TIP**
>
> • Identify programs that afford students academic and life experiences in other countries. Know if an international alumni base exists to support these programs.
>
> • Build relationships with program advisers and faculty who have lasting ties to international alumni.
>
> • Encourage alumni, parents and friends around the world to support students participating in local programs.

According to IGL's founding executive director, Sherman Teichman, IGL's alumni are a "vibrant, highly acclaimed and ethical set of leaders. From Day 1, our students are meeting alumni overseas."[29] The program is nurtured by a strong commitment from alumni to provide an excellent experience for undergraduates. "We are considered an intellectual Outward Bound program," states Teichman. The IGL orientation exercises are psychologically difficult, and students rely on each other in problem-solving, much like they do throughout the year as they research, debate and engage in dialogue about world affairs. The 20 distinct programs of IGL offer students a chance to "weave" their experience throughout more than one program and thereby interact with their peers on multiple levels and in various situations both on campus and abroad.

Tufts IGL alumni and students work together in numerous ways, including these:

- Alumni throughout the world are engaged through social entrepreneurship and alleviation efforts.
- Alumni at the U.S. Institute of Peace serve as advisers for an annual symposium.
- Tufts alumnus Jake Sherman, associate director for peacekeeping and security sector reform at the New York University Center on International Cooperation, was a guest speaker at the IGL's 2010 annual EPIIC international symposium. He is also convening a professional workshop on counterinsurgency in South Asia for the Tufts students.
- A senior lawyer in New York City provides internships on women and gender issues for a welfare and legal rights center.
- A recent alumnus who started an NGO in northern Uganda is helping create internships to support demobilized child soldiers and refugees.

The IGL is a model program, and universities and other organizations look to Tufts for advice on how to start similar programs. The U.S. Military Academies have new formal linkages with the IGL through Tufts' Alliance Linking Leaders in Education and the Services (ALLIES) program.

Today, 94 students from 15 countries (such as Rwanda, Singapore, China) and 17 universities participate in one of the hallmark IGL programs, the Tufts Initiative for Leadership and International Perspective. Started in 1998, this educational exchange program results in a cross-cultural educational exchange for students of various universities. The success of the program has garnered the attention and support of the Clinton Global Initiative.

Tufts alumni, many based overseas, care about the future welfare of all the programs of the IGL. There are also non-alumni members on the IGL Board of Directors. These are highly influential international figures and policymakers who have advised the program in the past. "Our alumni are engaged in an endowment drive to support the teaching program of IGL," says Teichman. "Without the alumni it would be incontestably highly impossible because we have a neural network ... which, to me, is like an intellectual microwave popcorn."

Business Schools

Max M. Fisher College of Business at the Ohio State University

The Max M. Fisher College of Business at the Ohio State University was founded in 1916. The school, located on the OSU campus, enrolls more than 5,600 students, almost 5,000 of whom are undergraduates.

The number of addressable alumni is approximately 62,000, with 966 (or 1.5 percent of the total) representing both undergraduate and graduate business alumni from 82 different countries. The international alumni program at Fisher relies on close communication and coordinated efforts across the university. Seven advancement staff members work with OSU's international alumni and the school's 29 international OSU alumni clubs organized by country. Some of the international clubs are led by Fisher grads. The school works closely with OSU's central alumni association as well as with development officers who have regular contact with international alumni. Director of Alumni Relations Michelle Jacobson and Executive Director of International Programs Melissa Torres provided an overview of some of the ways Fisher is giving its alumni abroad a reason to stay interested and involved in the life of its students and the school.[30] Here, then is Fisher's top 10 list of best practices for interactions between students and alumni:

1. The Elective Trek is a noncredit program for small groups of students (up to 20) who, under the guidance of a faculty member, study how a functional area of business operates overseas (e.g., textile distribution from India). Fisher's international alumni get involved by underwriting costs of trips, participating in the local programs or identifying business locations for appropriate site visits and assisting with local arrangements. Alumni have networking events with students and faculty involved in the Elective Trek experience. The Fisher staff members publicize these receptions in the school's quarterly newsletter.

   The Elective Trek is open to any student at the business school. Undergraduates, part-time and doctoral students have each contributed to this unique opportunity for cross-fertilization of ideas and contacts.

2. As alumni are involved with students in a field study, they are also typically helping Fisher by making local arrangements for the field experience and/or by sponsoring some of the expenses incurred during the program.

3. Fisher alumni also greet outbound exchange students. For example, as Fisher students prepared to go to Singapore recently, local alumni provided an orientation to the city. In addition, the students are invited to join the events hosted by the international alumni club. An OSU football game via satellite is a very popular fall social event.

4. Conversely, alumni also host dinners for inbound exchange programs. International alumni will schedule a send-off dinner for new students from their city before they leave for Columbus as well as informational dinners for prospective Fisher students.

5. International Fisher alumni represent the school at recruitment fairs.

6. The alumni have also been judges for the International CIBER Case Challenge, which from 2006 to 2010 was hosted by Fisher and held in Columbus. Undergraduates from Fisher and 15 other schools (12 from the United States and four from overseas) participate in this competition for undergraduate students. Fisher is home to a Center for International Business Education and Research (CIBER), which is one of the critically important vehicles used to globalize students, faculty and members of the business community who participate in their programs, and it provides an impetus to create and maintain a wide variety of programs. Melissa Torres has been instrumental in helping Fisher increase engagement between students and alumni through CIBER programs.

7. International alumni are resources for career placement leads and internships.

8. The state of Ohio has a new strategic plan for its public universities, which includes targeted goals for OSU to increase international placements abroad and increase international student enrollment. As part of this effort, Fisher invites alumni from any and all Ohio public universities in a particular country to attend a reception at the U.S. Embassy there. The idea met with success in 2009, when OSU President Gordon Gee took a trip to Warsaw, Poland, with the alumni relations office, at which time the U.S. Embassy hosted a reception for alumni from Ohio colleges and universities. By expanding the opportunity to all, the reception costs were spread across participating schools and attendance was bolstered.

9. Back on campus, Fisher sponsors a Distinguished International Speaker Series, which allows speakers to share their experiences with Fisher graduate students and faculty members over an informal luncheon. Alumni are often the speakers and are always invited to take part in the programs. Generally there are eight to 10 presentations per academic year. Previous speaker topics included the challenges and opportunities for expanding business in China, the impact of immigrant homebuyers on the market, the Hong Kong business environment, and the ways in which Japanese investment links Japan to China and Korea, including how political and historical tensions are managed.

10. Finally, the Fisher Frequent Flyer Fund was developed in response to the more challenging economic climate of 2009. Alumni are invited to donate frequent flyer miles for a student participating in an exchange program. Fisher may match the donor with an exchange student coming to his country. Alumni do not receive a tax deduction for this gift.

Fisher College is optimistic about the future of its international alumni programs. Alumni evaluations from the Elective Trek and exchange programs show that alumni have been satisfied with their experiences. The staff wants to continue to embrace innovation and to try new programs. "We have been afforded the luxury of trying things that didn't work well … we can approach alumni and invite them to participate and give their opinion," states Torres.

The open style of communication between alumni and the school is a source of pride for the school. "The level of openness of having international alumni involved is unique," continues Torres. The "best practices" list shows that alumni have many significant opportunities to interact with the students. Fisher alumni do more than just refer students to jobs.

Overall, OSU expects a long-term relationship with all its alumni and is committed to helping Fisher maintain its global connections as it provides a richness and diversity for the university as a whole. "OSU forges a deep connection with its students, and international alumni are no different," summarized Torres. "All we have to do is look for ways for them to get involved."

Graziadio School of Business and Management at Pepperdine University

The Graziadio School of Business and Management was founded in 1969 in Malibu, California. The school enrolls about 1,900 students a year, with over 75 percent attending an evening or weekend part-time executive program across five campuses in Southern California and one additional campus in the Northern California city of Santa Clara. The other students are full-time MBA candidates. Most of the international students are part of this cohort (40 percent of the current MBA class are international). In turn, outreach to international alumni occurs with the MBA degree-holders only.

Nicole Hall, executive director of alumni relations and career services, came to Graziadio in 2001 as the director of career services. In her first four years, she worked with the alumni relations department and frequently interacted with alumni who were involved in both helping students find jobs and helping the school build a presence in its regional community. At this time the alumni relations staff was also charged with fundraising. Thus, it could seem to a graduate that his or her alumni involvement with the school was on several different levels. In 2005, alumni relations and career services decided to merge offices, a move that resulted in a combined calendar of events and a much better resourced, larger department. In 2008, alumni relations officers separated out their development roles to create gift officers who worked solely with prospects and fundraising. Today, Hall's team focuses on providing a combination of career services, support and alumni relations programs. From her team, one FTE works with MBA alumni (including the international body) and a number of staff members devote some percentage of their time to international programs and outreach, enough to equal an additional FTE.

While in the early stages of having programs for international alumni, Graziadio realized the benefits of collaboration. The business school has relationships with more than 20 international schools for study abroad programs. Hall and her staff work with the global program office by identifying local alumni who may connect with the students studying in their city or region. By doing so, the alumni relations and career services staff play a role in supporting students during what may be a challenging time of transition.

With more than 26,000 of the total 32,000 business school alumni resident in California, the staff expends most of its resources in the state. However, outside California Graziadio partners closely with the university's central alumni relations office and its regional chapters. Alumni from the business school are full-fledged members of the Pepperdine University chapters in Asia Pacific, Germany, London, Shanghai and South Korea. Membership in these university chapters spans across all schools. "They are not as structured as stateside chapters," says Hall. "We try to do a very good job on the university and business school level to leverage deans and faculty travel schedules to provide programming opportunities to our chapters outside of California and the United States."[31] When asked which department takes the lead on the events occurring overseas, Hall replies that the main speaker dictates the organizing office; for example, invitations for the university president's trip to London will come from the central alumni relations office. On the other hand, Graziadio's Paris alumni have been very active since 2007. With the dean making annual trips to Paris, Hall's team is the go-to department for invitations and the RSVP list. Even

---

TIP

- Merging career services and alumni relations provides efficiency and a centralized mechanism for involving international alumni in student experiences and job placements.

- Partnering with other business school study-abroad programs provides students with opportunities for global study.

- Communicating regularly with international alumni about the international demographics provides an important context for their involvement with students and with each other.

- Ask international alumni to join conference calls with individual MBA students. Share realities about working and living overseas. Maintain this personal approach.

with a heavy business school–centric event such as that in Paris, the alumni from all schools will be invited to attend.

Pepperdine believes in the power of a personal approach. The full-time MBA alumni relations officer's strategy for e-communications includes communicating with international alumni about the demographics of the incoming MBA class (rankings, geographic profile) as well as sharing alumni promotions and milestones for each graduating class. Knowing that their staff is not going to travel internationally on a regular basis, there is a large emphasis placed on connecting with others via the school's online community and other social media.

Hall and her staff believe the base metric of evaluation is ensuring the alumni contact information is both current and utilized. In addition, with a large percentage of their MBA alumni abroad, the school has noticed more alumni each year helping to recruit MBA students (a fast-growing trend in Asia). "I would also want to see that our percent of engaged international alumni was increasing over time," explains Hall. The goal is to chart an annual increase across all levels of engagement.

In the near future (and considering the current economic climate of 2010), the school will invest more time and resources to support their e-communications strategy. These include customizing the online community to include communities for different graduate programs, developing career-related webinars for alumni abroad, and extending an invitation to more alumni to participate in conference calls with students. In this scenario, the office of alumni relations and career services sponsors a call between an international alumnus and a current MBA student. The alumni help the students prepare for interviews with firms headquartered overseas and help them translate important cultural differences.

Creating opportunities for international alumni to become more engaged with prospective or current students brings alumni close to their alma mater in ways in which they learn about current academic and co-curricular programs as well as their alumni community at large. Alumni overseas care deeply about the reputation of their college or university and they know too well that well-publicized rankings and positive (or poor) press can quickly change public opinion.

"Private" opinion is also important. An alumnus's positive feelings will spread to his or her family, friends, business and other social networks. Providing more than one way for alumni abroad to reconnect with the campus is going to be a way to influence these opinions.

ENDNOTES

23. Booth interview, June 10, 2009.

24. Walker email, Feb. 9, 2011.

25. Kathy Lord, interview with author, New York City, Sept. 15, 2009.

26. Woodall interview, July 13, 2009.

27. Teo Choo Soo, telephone interview with author, July 13, 2009.

28. Jose Luis de Cea, telephone interview with author, Oct. 9, 2009.

29. Sherman Teichman, interview with author, Oct. 13, 2009.

30. Melissa Torres and Michelle Jacobson, telephone interview with author, Aug. 6, 2009.

31. Nicole Hall, telephone interview with author, Sept. 4, 2009.

PROGRAMMING WITH FACULTY

Independent Schools

Benenden School

Benenden faculty travel with alumni office officials to regional groups around the world. Senior faculty members have a long history at the school and a strong sense of what it means to engage alumni. The outreach programs started in the 1980s and the 1990s with Hong Kong. Senior faculty would be recognized and thanked by the school for their service and sent to Hong Kong as a way to learn the student culture.

Today, faculty traveling on school holidays to key alumni communities may attract an audience of more than students. For example, faculty on a recent Easter break offered to meet alumni. Faculty proactively approached the alumni office to coordinate alumni visits, meals and, with more active help from the development staff, some events. The costs to support these gatherings are minimal, considering the positive outcomes of having a current faculty member engage with alumni, parents and students.

> **TIP**
>
> - Invest in faculty travel. Encourage faculty to travel internationally to learn the culture of their current students.
> - Provide adequate financial support for faculty visits. Set expectations about the type of events they will attend, meetings they will host and alumni they will specifically cultivate.

Colleges and Universities

Imperial College London

Imperial College London launched the International Ambassador scheme in September 2006 to enhance the way in which Imperial engaged with its international alumni. With one-third of its 105,000 contactable alumni living outside the U.K., this new and exclusive program was another way for the college to strategically celebrate its 100th anniversary while also leveraging the time and talent of its faculty and senior administrators. With support from the rector and his administration and faculty, the alumni office matched faculty travel with international alumni programming opportunities to produce what has become an integral annual program for international alumni, winning a CASE Circle of Excellence silver award in 2008.

The key players in this program include the alumni office staff, the international alumni groups, the ambassadors themselves (the rector, pro rectors and faculty) and their personal assistants (PAs). During the inaugural year, a common information system, called the ambassador database, was developed as a means for Imperial's departments and staff to track overseas travel. PAs would enter tentative or confirmed schedules into the database, and staff could see a report on where an academic would be traveling and which days might be available for an alumni event. Automating these logistics worked well during the first year. The alumni office had access to information early enough to contact the overseas group with a proposal of a college speaker and a possible date or two. The hard part of identifying speakers and dates was accomplished

> **TIP**
>
> • Develop a method of tracking faculty travel. The method should be available both to academic departments and to the alumni relations office.
>
> • State expectations from the beginning. For example, all ambassador travel is covered by the ambassadors' own budgets.
>
> • Plan appropriate ways of thanking ambassadors.

in this first step. All travel and accommodation for the ambassadors was covered by the ambassador's own budget, this being an important premise of the scheme. The senior academic and administrative leaders recognized their role and the responsibility of building relationships with alumni. Knowing how important it was for the college to bring its centenary celebration across the world, alumni groups enthusiastically welcomed the opportunity to host an ambassador in 2006–2007.

Imperial has also recognized the importance of allowing the program to change over time. During subsequent years of the program, the staff has eliminated the use of the ambassador database in favor of personal appeals to the rector, pro rectors and faculty. Today, the rector (chief executive officer), the pro rectors (senior administrators and deans) and faculty principals (department chairs) are all involved. The alumni office prepares an event brief for each ambassador that provides the overall objectives for the regional events, background information about the hosting club and its key volunteers and a detailed overview of the event logistics and timeline, providing both the ambassador and the hosting group with all the necessary information for the event so they can feel reassured that events will run well and unnecessary distractions are eliminated. Some alumni office staff will attend events as well in order to provide on-site assistance and to continue to assess the effectiveness of this overseas program.

The alumni office has placed great importance on thanking the ambassadors and their PAs and has tried a numbers of ways to do so, including post-event debriefings, formal thank-you notes and hosting a superlative-type awards ceremony ("for participating in the longest event"), which further builds on the camaraderie among the group.[32]

International ambassadors will continue to make alumni feel connected and informed about the college and the important role they play in its future. The program provides an excellent tool for alumni chapter or group management. More established groups may use an event to recruit new volunteers and more lapsed, struggling groups may use an ambassador visit as impetus for reviving their activities.

Key ingredients for this program's future success include ongoing institutional support, an engaged faculty, responsive and enthusiastic alumni, as well as a workable and flexible plan to best direct the energies of all parties involved.

London School of Economics

Focusing on continued improvement and effectiveness, the staff at the London School of Economics (LSE) believes the ideal time to survey alumni is every three years. It is the ideal time to work on enhancing an existing program and evaluating the effectiveness of the program with the alumni body.

Charlotte Armah, LSE's head of alumni relations and a former management consultant, looks at managing the program in the way she used to manage a portfolio by asking about the program's purpose. "Does it match the needs of the alumni? If it doesn't we can discard the program." She continues, "For example, the focus on entrepreneurship program was going on for five years. This was an annual event for graduates and for alumni less than five years out. Alumni pitched business ideas in front of judges, and we've been able to fill a room with 400 people."[33] Interest in this program declined, continues Armah. "Student societies are now interested in career networking, and the career office has supported these students." This example is one in which the return on investment was not there when other offices were serving this niche for the alumni and students.

TIP

- Ask faculty to add a day to their busy travel schedules. Eliminate as many potential conflicts with their existing schedules as possible.

- Alumni relations does not always have to foot the bill. When faculty members are speaking to alumni groups, they are providing great publicity for the school. Seek additional funds from affiliated departments for expenses associated with faculty travel.

Deciding to try something new, LSE now focuses on faculty visits. Modeled after the Imperial College Ambassador Scheme (originated by LSE's director of development and alumni relations, Fiona Kirk), this program is different in that faculty are asked to add a day to their travel schedules in order to attend alumni programs and provide remarks. The LSE staff has requested extra funding from the external relations department to cover the costs of an extra day of accommodations and meals for the faculty member. The financial support for faculty is a good incentive and relieves the alumni group of any responsibility to fund the visit. Kirk believes this model is a good business practice for LSE. "At our U.K. university we try to follow practices of the U.S.," says Kirk.[34]

Business Schools

Anderson School of Management, UCLA

For the Anderson School of Management, another strategic decision has been made to support faculty travel. The alumni relations office receives additional funding in its budget for faculty travel, both domestic and abroad. Through a semi-annual travel survey (see figure 3.2) faculty members learn that:

> The Offices of the Faculty Chair, the Dean, and Alumni Relations are working together to maximize the presence of our faculty members as you travel the world. This is a voluntary program in which we work with you to identify opportunities for you to connect with our alumni when you travel.

> The Dean's office will award faculty participants $500–$1000 to offset costs of travel (depending on travel location) when we successfully coordinate an alumni event.

The programs add considerable value to the social activities taking place abroad. As alumni in Brazil attest, "We like the idea of having faculty spend an extra day to see alumni."[35]

As it considers its future engagement of international alumni, former alumni relations executive director Bob Pettit believes the school is achieving its goals and experiencing growth every year. Faculty members are traveling and staff members are also seeing more interaction with students during their time at Anderson. Pettit and his team met with international grads, before they left Los Angeles, to inquire about their home or work locations, hoping to have their help with chapters in places of strategic interest such as Asia.

TIP

- Develop an electronic version of a semi-annual travel survey.
- Provide a travel stipend to faculty only after event logistics are confirmed.

FIG. 3.2 | ANDERSON SCHOOL OF MANAGEMENT TRAVEL SURVEY

UCLAAnderson
alumni network

Faculty Travel Survey (Q1, FY 09-10)

1. TRAVEL PLANS

The Offices of the Faculty Chair, the Dean, and Alumni Relations are working together to maximize the presence of our faculty members as you travel the world. This is a voluntary program in which we work with you to identify opportunities for you to connect with our alumni when you travel.

The Dean's office will award faculty participants $500 - $1000 to offset costs of travel (depending on travel location) when we successfully coordinate an alumni event. More details are available in two documents: (1) Faculty Alumni Outreach Policy and (2) Faculty Alumni Processing Procedures.

Thank you for taking a few moments to answer the 6 questions below.

★ 1. Contact Information:

Name

Email Address

2. Major Academic Conferences

Please specify the names and dates (if known) of the major annual/recurring conferences for your area(s) of academic expertise:

Accounting

Decisions, Operations & Technology Management

Finance

Global Economics and Management

HR and Organizational Behavior

Information Systems

Interdisciplinary Group in Behavioral Decision Making

Marketing

Policy

Other (please specify)

3. Domestic Travel

Please enter dates for any known travel to the following domestic destinations:

Exit this survey

Boston

Chicago

Dallas

Denver

Hawaii

Las Vegas

New York

Orange County

Phoenix

Portland

San Diego

San Francisco Bay Area

Santa Barbara/ Ventura

Seattle

Washington D.C.

Other (please specify)

4. International Travel

Please enter dates for any known travel to the following international destinations:

Argentina

Brazil

Chile

China

France

India

Japan

Mexico

Singapore

Spain

What remains most important for Anderson is that the school took a strategic view and organized the alumni board. The dean started traveling overseas to meet with alumni who shared their desires for a greater connection to the school. Staff worked quickly within a 12-month planning cycle to develop international chapters. The combination of board development, high-level outreach and faculty engagement is what Anderson is banking on to sustain regional efforts for the near future. Next stop on their itinerary: Brazil and Chile.

Faculty speakers are probably some of the most popular programs for your alumni. Along with creating ambassadors and disseminating a travel survey, identify the campus departments involved with international academic programs and begin to discuss the benefits of working together. The faculty may not be as well-known, but requesting an opportunity to sit in on their classes and/or meeting with them to discuss their work are both ways to find out more about them.

ENDNOTES

32. Information from email correspondence with Louise Birrell, alumni events and marketing manager, Communications and Development Division, Imperial College London, Jan. 13, 2011.

33. Armah interview.

34. Fiona Kirk, telephone interview with author, July 6, 2009.

35. Quotation from interview with professional staff, Westwood, CA, Aug. 3, 2009.

SIGNATURE PROGRAMS

Independent Schools

Practice #1: Interesting and Meaningful Publications

The areas of alumni affairs, communications and marketing must collaborate on successful publications. Publishing features with a local angle helps celebrate the nostalgia that alumni have for their time on campus. Many alumni have not been back to their school or the region since graduation. Run stories about the area, the school and the people they might remember. Additionally, continuing to promote the larger international alumni network in hard-copy publications and on the web reinforces your school's globalism.

Singapore American School does just this. Opened in 1956 by a group of American parents, the Singapore American School (SAS) serves the expatriate community in Singapore. Started in a house with seven teachers and 98 students, the school has grown to more than 330 teachers and 3,800 students. SAS has thousands of alumni around the world. The largest groups of alumni are concentrated in the United States, primarily in Texas, California and New York.

Lauren Thomas, former associate director of alumni relations for SAS, explains the school's strategy: "The strategic plan recognizes the importance of creating a comprehensive alumni relations program that engages alumni in the life of the school. In 2006, SAS celebrated its 50th anniversary and welcomed hundreds of alumni back to campus. In the run-up to this major event, the school created an office of development/advancement, which included a focus on alumni relations. At that time, an alumni database and web site were set up and plans were made to engage alumni in the 50th anniversary celebrations."[36]

Thomas adds that in the 2007–2008 school year, "the development office added a staff member to coordinate further alumni programs and enhance the communications from the school to the alumni. SAS provides useful content for alumni, since most have not been back to Singapore for years." Publications include plenty of Singapore angles. "The alumni office–provided content often leads to conversations between alumni about something that is dear to them and increases interaction with the life of the school," says Thomas.

Another example from Singapore comes from UWCSEA. The staff likes to incorporate a piece of the school's curriculum in their alumni outreach and programs. On their campus, UWCSEA students are required to participate in value-added, co-curricular programs under the auspices of Social Service and Global Concerns, which are particular areas of emphasis reflected in the school's mission and vision. According to the staff, many alumni carry out these principles in their life after graduation as founders of NGOs or as volunteers in their local or international communities. "Values in Practice" is a regular column in UWCSEA's magazine, *One North*. Alumni are recognized for their service and are featured here and on its website.

In addition to running stories about a school's region and alumni profiles, school magazines might consider using key anniversaries to engage alumni at a distance. Turning 100 years old, an anniversary of becoming co-educational or a milestone within the alumni office or alumni community (e.g., the 5,000th registered online community member) are all stories to leverage and expand upon.

Founded more than 560 years ago, the U.K.'s Eton College has a long history to uphold and share with its alumni. Of the 15,000 "Old Etonians," 1,500 live overseas. Although Eton continues to be very much a British school and does not recruit internationally, about 10 percent of its current students are from abroad (some may hold more than one passport).

"Britian's colonial past has meant that Old Etonians could be found around the world," explains Jackie Tarrant-Barton, clerk to the Old Etonian Association.[37] "Our members have been in the habit of meeting in major cities around the globe for over a century." The Fourth of June, the school's traditional holiday, is a popular day for these Old Etonian gatherings.

Today, staff at Eton actively encourage and support these alumni events. Eton publishes a list of international contacts on its website and in its alumni publications. A small removable insert in the middle of Eton's magazine, the *Eton College Chronicle*, lists international contacts alongside alumni societies (or shared interest groups) and a calendar of events for the entire year. "By highlighting our international events in our publications, it reinforces what an interesting place Eton is. We are perpetuating our 'brand.' It's not just for those who live abroad—it's also for 90 percent that live in the U.K.," says Eton's Development Director Bill O'Hearn.[38]

Practice #2: Annual Events for Young Alumni and Other Key Classes

Younger alumni have needs and interests that may be leveraged in a positive way to build a stronger relationship between themselves and their school. UWCSEA hosted its first Young Alumni Reunion in Singapore in 2007 during the December holiday break, when many college students were home visiting family. The response in 2007 was less than expected, since in an effort to accommodate teachers the event was held too early for some of the returning alumni. In 2008, the event was held later in the month, and the response improved. This event attracted college students returning home for the holidays as well as young alumni working in Singapore. In addition to the Young Alumni Reunion, a formal program was started in August 2008 for alumni of UWCSEA who were 30, 20 and10 years post-graduation. The school felt this was a phenomenal success, attracting almost 300 alumni from 32 countries.

Practice #3: Scholarships from International Alumni Donors

Hong Kong International School (HKIS) educates more than 2,600 students a year on two campuses in Hong Kong. More than 50 percent of the students are U.S. citizens. Founded in 1966 with the assistance of the Lutheran Church–Missouri Synod, the school's mission statement encourages students and teachers to "dedicate their minds to inquiry." In addition, HKIS identifies six areas, called Student Learning Results (SLRs), that provide a framework for students to strive for fuller academic, spiritual and character development.

In support of the SLRs (specifically, "self-motivated learning" and "contributing to society") and to help further the school's mission, HKIS and overseas alumni Desmond Chu '91 and Kenneth Koo '79 established the James A. Handrich Service Leadership Endowment, in honor of Associate Head of School James (Jim) A. Handrich, who retired in July 2007. As the endowment's website states, Handrich served as the elementary school principal, high school principal, interim head of school and associate head of school over the course of his 24 years with HKIS.

In 2008, the endowment began to support student service learning projects. Student groups received up to US$10,000. The school's 2007–2008 annual report lists the three groups of seniors awarded funds from the endowment for the following senior projects:

- Documentary about poverty and social injustice in Cambodia
- Documentary about the volunteer experience in Kolkata, India
- Fundraising to help build a water project in Yunan, China (partnering with Concordia Welfare and Education Foundation)

It is worth noting that each project focused on issues outside Hong Kong.

The Handrich Service Leadership Endowment is being promoted to all alumni. With the vast majority of alumni living outside of Hong Kong, the current and future benefactors of this valuable student scholarship will be international alumni.

Practice #4: Regional Events Where Everyone Is Invited

The ways in which international alumni are invited to events is also an important consideration. At Exeter, one regional group hosts the event and invites alumni in nearby countries to attend.

For Benenden, all regional events are open to the families of alumni. For example, at the school's events in Bangkok, it is customary for parents and grandparents to participate. A few years ago, more than 200 people attended a school-sponsored sailing cruise. Extending invitations to families signifies the great respect the school has for the families who sent their children to Benenden. The expectation that extended families will be included in regional events is prevalent throughout Asia.

Practice #5: Mentoring and Post-Graduation Programs for Alumni

The UWCSEA staff has been asking itself, "What's left to do?" The school has an active web portal, an alumni magazine, an electronic newsletter and a reunion program. Now it has started adding services—specifically, a volunteer program for its alumni. Started in January 2009, the volunteer program builds on what is referred to as a gap year, which is offered for graduating UWCSEA students who wish to take a year off after graduation to work as a volunteer in an established program. Alumni can either take time to volunteer in a similar program or they can offer volunteer opportunities to other alumni. The UWCSEA staff will be evaluating whether their current staffing levels can sustain the volunteer program and similar new services.

Practice #6: Don't Forget Your Mascot

The American School in London (ASL) sponsored a traveling mascot program that has their mascot, Eagle, traveling around the world, visiting alumni and sharing his experiences through an online travel blog, *Wingin' It.*

Eagle has visited diverse locales such as Niagara Falls, Atlanta, New Mexico, Stratford-upon-Avon, Massachusetts, Qatar, Pennsylvania, Chicago, New Zealand, New Hampshire, the Caribbean, Plymouth Rock, Tokyo, Moscow, Oslo, Seoul, San Francisco and Shanghai.

Alumni have a started a waiting list for Eagle. The program has generated enthusiasm and worldwide participation for ASL.[39]

Colleges and Universities

Practice #1: An Alumni Book Series

Founded in 1963, the Chinese University of Hong Kong (CUHK) is a comprehensive research university with a global vision and a mission to combine tradition with modernity and to bring together China and the West. More than 120,000 graduates are connected through some 90 alumni associations both within and outside Hong Kong, all of which are supported and closely linked through the alumni affairs office.

The CUHK Alumni Book Series is a creative initiative among overseas alumni to foster ties to CUHK and to provide service to the communities. The alumni affairs office coordinates production of each publication, and overseas alumni associations take charge of the editorial and creative aspects of the project. Director of Alumni Affairs Antonia Yeung explains that the project is entirely supported by alumni donations. Proceeds from the sale of the publications go toward Baby Bamboo Operation, a charitable cause overseen by Federation of CUHK Alumni Associations' Education Foundation that benefits education of children in China.

Since 2000, a number of overseas alumni associations have published a volume in the CUHK Alumni Book Series to share their stories and experiences of living overseas and maintain a connection to CUHK. "It signifies the spirit and the solidarity of our alumni around the globe," Yeung states.[40]

- *Our New York Experience: Voices from the CUHK Alumni* (2000)
- *The CUHK Alumni in San Francisco Bay Area* (2006)
- *Under the Rockies: Life Stories of CUHK Alumni in Calgary* (2008)
- *Along the Shores of Lake Ontario: CUHK Alumni in Toronto* (2009)
- *CUHK Alumni in Southern California* (2009)
- *Cherry Blossom Memories: CUHK Alumni in Japan* (2009)

The success of the CUHK Alumni Book Series can be described by four salient features.

1. Full alumni participation from different generations and locales. From conceptualization, drafting and editing to promotion, the publication is made possible by the concerted effort of alumni in a region. Authors include CUHK alumni from as early as the 1950s (graduates from the founding colleges of CUHK, predating the establishment of the university). The series has consistently received an overwhelming response from overseas alumni. Since its inception, more than 200 alumni have submitted personal stories, images of artwork and photos to the publications. CUHK students on exchange in the areas concerned have also been invited to share their unique experiences.

2. Real-life stories and impact of the CUHK experience. All articles in the publications portray real-life stories and achievements of CUHK alumni in their new homelands. Topics include memorable college tales, important life events and cultural adaptation overseas. The alumni authors often recount the people who have played important roles in their lives: hostel roommates, best friends and spouses, as well as professors and mentors who have helped shape them. The publications also feature the history and achievements of alumni associations in the various areas.

In recognition of the considerable efforts from all alumni involved, the CUHK vice chancellor or director of alumni affairs, and the premier, mayor, or legislative councilors of the local region contribute prefaces to the publications.

3. Mission with a formidable cause. The book project has evolved from an effort to promote alumni fellowship, an album in celebration of the alumni associations' anniversaries, to a cross-region collaboration to present a collection of at least 10 books published under the series to commemorate the 50th anniversary of the university in 2013. In addition, as mentioned above, proceeds from sales are donated to Baby Bamboo Operation.

4. Enhancement of visibility and promotion of goodwill. Each publication is widely distributed to local universities, libraries and related bodies, both as a means to promote the goodwill of CUHK and the alumni and as a unique source of information about the cultural history of overseas Chinese. Some media outlets have reported on the book series. The publication is also widely distributed to all CUHK overseas alumni associations and sister institutions for their interest.

Publications released in 2010 and 2011 include books from Victoria, Australia; Calgary, British Columbia (2nd edition); Greater New York; and Northern California.

Practice #2: Serving Alumni Needs

Great salespeople know their product inside and out. Marketers understand consumer behavior. When you combine the two in advancement and have professionals with both an in-depth knowledge base of their institution and a keen understanding of the alumni, all parties win. At the Massachusetts Institute of Technology, Lou Alexander, director of alumni education, is the person who has attended to relationships abroad.

During his 30 years at MIT, Alexander has held a number of positions and traveled extensively across Europe. He was assigned to build the MIT alumni network in Europe in 1993, a job he continued to do for 10 years. For MIT, alumni models did not exist overseas the way they did in the United States. "The idea was to have a high concentration of clubs in a small geographic territory where we can leverage larger populations (similar to U.S. states or major cities)," explains Alexander.[41] In some regions, such as Latin America, this approach was difficult because of "small alumni populations and a large geographic space," adds Alexander.

When Alexander began his role, MIT had 12 alumni clubs outside the United States and only a few were active. For the first few years, his job was to work on getting to know others, providing outreach to alumni abroad, and recruiting more volunteers.

"What really set the tone was what we did in Switzerland. This helped us gel in a different way," he says. In the early 1990s, about 75 percent of the MIT alumni in Europe were alumni from the school's graduate programs, which meant that Alexander needed to coordinate events that were far different from nostalgia-based programs.

Another factor was the economy. Educated white collar employees were losing jobs in Europe in the mid-1990s. Even Switzerland had problems. Alexander responded by creating a program "of value" for the alumni. After a year of listening to alumni share their professional goals, Alexander and the local alumni identified a real barrier to preparing for a recession was technology transfer and lack of access to information. Spurred by what he had learned during the process, Alexander met with an MIT contact, who had a model for technology transfer, and a Swiss venture capitalist. The outcome was a joint panel of MIT alumni and non-alumni discussing the tech transfer process and ways the Swiss economy could benefit. Alexander's theme: they approached an issue of professional concern and billed it as an MIT program, but facilitated in a Swiss way.

Going forward, Alexander and the alumni have tried to engage each other on issues where countries and MIT alumni can benefit. "The individual cultures are extremely important, and you should have tailored programs to each culture," says Alexander. "Today we have 12 active clubs: Norway, Germany, France, Belgium/Netherlands, Great Britain, Ireland, Switzerland, Spain, Portugal, Italy, Greece and Turkey." MIT has also hosted European Club workshops (and included Sweden and Israel for training purposes). During these workshops, Alexander took a backseat role and let the peers talk about what was happening with their groups. Some cultures did not know what *volunteerism* meant. At night, outside the formal program, Alexander would meet with these alumni who would benefit from some additional training. Dedication to a region helped MIT build a solid foundation in Europe.

During his 10 years of working in Europe, Alexander evaluated his efforts by comparing dollars raised and the percentage of alumni participants. Giving increased by 120 percent during this time period. Before 1993, 18 percent of all alumni in Europe made donations; this number grew by 1,000 alumni in 2003 and the participation rate rose to 26 percent. A few years ago, another 600 donors had been added to the rolls in Europe, bringing the participation rate to 28 percent. At the time of this writing, more than 6,000 alumni reside in Europe (compared to 5,000 in 2003). "We have not done anything different in asking for contributions. Alumni are giving," says Alexander.

As director of alumni education, Alexander is working world-wide with senior alumni to build programs with content, and not based on nostalgia. He continues to remember his Switzerland model as he plans programs to meet today's needs of MIT's diverse alumni body. "The key to understanding cultural differences is listening and not coming in with a pre-formed template in mind. Listen to volunteers and try to be respectful of culture and how they handle matters."

Alexander also suggests trying to fashion programs that fit the capabilities of the volunteers to ensure that everyone involved feels good about their efforts. In Europe, he encouraged groups to conduct events in conjunction with other alumni groups.

He also tends to involve more senior alumni to gain access to a meeting space. Alexander looks up giving records and makes introductions when on the road. He thanks donors for their gifts, explains how the MIT alumni association works and asks alumni to get more involved in the events. "This is usually successful," he says.

Reciprocal arrangements work as well. In Norway, Anderson Consulting Group saw that the alumni clubs were working on programs that were relevant to the world and wanted to partner with MIT to sponsor faculty travel to Norway. Together they produced annual speaker events. Anderson Consulting Group could invite employees and local clients to hear from MIT professors, and in turn, the small MIT alumni population in Norway could have a larger networking opportunity at the co-sponsored events. The company and the university both benefitted.

Today the programming model continues. A View from the Top is a series of programs rolled out in 2009 that leverages MIT's elite alumni network. For the London program, Alexander asked heads of companies to host a program covering the world financial crisis. The program was taped, made available online, and engaged the larger university community. As one observer of international education programs said, "It is a high-touch, high-end program."[42]

Like others in the field, Alexander is rethinking the role of alumni chapters. "Our goal is to become coaches. I want to see who is out there," says Alexander. He believes clubs are generally most effective with younger people but that the alumni relations staff must then play a coaching role by identifying good volunteers and training them to lead groups.

"We need to get away from thinking that clubs are our main representatives in any city," says Alexander. As groups mature, alumni will naturally break off into other areas, such as community service.

Alexander spends a lot of time talking to regional development officers to strategize ways MIT can get alumni involved at a higher, institutional level. For example, he will go to New York City and have an evening discussion with a range of alumni from different backgrounds and ages. They discuss the impact MIT has in the city, and Alexander gets their thoughts on what the future issues are going to be for MIT. Alumni have a chance to react to these issues and discuss strategies for addressing these issues via high level programs. He wants to know who is available for speeches and who will provide information and access for alumni.

According to Alexander, the future of international alumni relations is becoming more decentralized and more flexible. "Think one year out with an eye on the second year," he advises. MIT is trying to take advantage of opportunities when they arise. Staying nimble has advantages. For example, MIT Germany asked for a professor to speak at its annual meeting. When Alexander suggested, "Look at your alumni," he was encouraging the leaders to recruit their own talent. In the end, the annual meeting organizers asked one of the View from the Top presenters in London to be the keynote speaker. He was joined by their alumni on a panel.

Getting international alumni to think regionally is a major change for MIT. "For so long, we have tried to make volunteers serve our needs rather than serve the needs of the volunteers," says Alexander. "We can engage them for short periods of time if we can fit in their scheme."

Short periods of engagement add up.

Practice #3: Coordinating Capital Campaigns

Stanford communicated its current campaign priorities via Leading Matters, a half-day program with the president, deans and faculty. The format consisted of an afternoon panel, evening cocktail hour and dinner followed by a multimedia show. Intentionally created to be low key (with no solicitation), these events attracted record numbers of attendees in the United States and in their international alumni "hubs," such as London.

Steve Suda (currently Stanford's managing director of international principal gifts) and the international division were the architects of the program. Suda invited campus departments and the alumni association staff to meetings held twice a month. "In summer, we went to each school and asked them for their input on their top international prospects. We had input from all the schools and were able to have a top list for fiscal year 2010," he says.[43] One of Suda's roles was to coordinate the cultivation and stewardship strategies of the entire core of development officers across campus. The process was transparent, as everyone involved had access to the campaign database and prospect files. "If there were multiple development officers vying for same prospect, the international division helped decide which development officer took the lead," Suda says.

Practice #4: Relationships with Consulates, Embassies and Community Organizations

"We have close relationships with Canadian consular staff," says Marie Earle, former associate vice president, alumni, at the University of British Columbia, and executive director of the UBC Alumni Association until 2010.[44] Consulates host send-off parties and other events for the university and have close ties to Canadian Chamber of Commerce offices. Additionally, building brand recognition for UBC is made much easier with the support from organizations such as Canada House in London and the Canadian embassy in Washington, D.C. "We can also partner with the Canadian organizations in major cities. It may work best for us because we're so small in Canada," adds Earle.

One such organization is Connect 2 Canada, a virtual network run from the Canadian embassy in Washington, D.C., which hosts information on alumni news and events. UBC publicizes the events, but consulate staff members usually provide a report on Canadian affairs during the program. The Canadian consulate will also co-sponsor events in smaller regions, such as San Francisco. UBC also makes use of the government-sponsored B.C. Alumni network, a web-based platform for alumni living in Asia who want to maintain contact with fellow UBC alumni and with the province. UBC publicizes events in the network's newsletter and gives profiles of local alumni in Asia.

Tufts' alumni relations office works closely with the Tufts' Fletcher School of Diplomacy alumni staff in identifying embassy venues in Washington, D.C., as well as abroad. With many Fletcher School graduates living and working overseas as representatives for the U.S. State Department or an NGO, opportunities to collaborate as program hosts exist each year.

Practice #5: Alumni Ambassadors for Alumni Relations

George Washington University's worldwide community includes 225,000 alumni in more than 150 countries. There are approximately 12,000 alumni living abroad with almost half in Asia and another third in Europe and the Middle East.

The university counts six active alumni chapters abroad, primarily in Asia (Korea, Taiwan, Beijing, Hong Kong, Turkey) and the U.K. and is working with nine additional evolving alumni chapters in Asia, the Middle East, Europe and Latin America.

In 2009, GW launched its Global Ambassador program. GW deputizes some highly engaged alumni, who regularly travel for business from the United States to Latin America and other areas, to be alumni ambassadors to meet with alumni in these cities. GW is using this alumni resource strategically. Director of International Alumni Relations Oksana Carlson explains: "We are unlikely to plan major programs in these areas. We provide alumni relations collateral and updates on the university. It has worked very well as a pilot because we carefully screen these ambassadors."[45]

Carlson believes the program is more focused on quality than quantity. "In most cases [these alumni] have been involved in the university in a major way, so when they go abroad for business, they can meet over a meal or drinks with the alumni," continues Carlson. These hand-picked proxies have a good understanding of the university, the priorities of the alumni office and how alumni engagement will help build worldwide community for GW.

With close to 6,000 alumni in Asia, GW is now exporting a reunion experience called the Global Forum, which takes place over a day and a half. While GW does have an alumni weekend at its campus in Washington, D.C., the Global Forum invites international alumni, parents, students and friends to meet within their region. Along with some typical social time, the 2009 conference featured 11 alumni and GW faculty experts who spoke on U.S. and Asia relations and about how different industries and sectors were being affected by the global recession and the prognosis for future stability. In Asia, therefore, "ambassadors" work alongside GW staff to help create awareness of both the program and the university as a whole. "They are our promoters," boasts Carlson.

Business Schools

Practice #1: Different Approaches to Reunion Programs

INSEAD has been hosting alumni reunions for 20 years. Classes return every five years. The alumni relations staff recruits one or more alumni to be a reunion chair (or co-chairs) to work on the social and logistical side of the reunion, encouraging attendance and participation. There are also often dozens of volunteers recruited by this chair (or co-chairs) who work in their region as country representatives to do the same. Similarly, the alumni fund staff members recruit one or more alumni to be reunion chair or co-chairs to raise money toward a class gift.

Building such geographic groups works well and encourages alumni to participate in the reunion weekends and give toward their class gift. The events generally take place on the Fontainebleau campus each spring and fall. Additionally, there is an Alumni Forum each November in Asia, which is open to all alumni. New for INSEAD are the one-year-after reunions. The school believes that such an event for recent graduates will yield high value in strengthening the bond between new alumni and INSEAD. INSEAD has designed a brand identity for its reunion programs (see figure 3.3). Now, alumni one year out and beyond will associate the same INSEAD logo with their reunion experience.

Marisa Cooke, INSEAD director of alumni affairs and the annual fund, and Craig McKenna, associate director of alumni relations and services, strive for "continuous improvement" with their work with alumni, and an alumni survey is issued regularly, generally every three years. Membership numbers in associations, event participation and donation rates are also tracked.

Staff also looks at ways to use new methods and modes of online tools to measure and evaluate. "When we start something new," says Cooke, "we will often put a focus group in place to get feedback. We're constantly trying to improve and innovate"[46]

When organizing the annual plans for the year, Cooke and McKenna try to build in some flexibility for innovation and the opportunity to respond to new requests or ideas. Annual plans are reviewed each year with the INSEAD Alumni Association and its executive committee, with special emphasis placed on this question: What can we achieve with our resources and how do we do it?

FIG. 3.3 | INSTEAD REUNION PROGRAM COVER

INSEAD

Alumni Reunion
Reconnecting with
the Business School
for the World

Altogether, it is evident that INSEAD's overall strategy as it applies to alumni relations is of central importance, and the staff helps translate high-level goals to specific action steps for alumni.

CONCLUSION

Signature programs from one school may become the "new thing" for another. The examples above include creative ways to engage constituents from around the world. Think about services currently offered at your institution: What could be enhanced? What will it cost to export a program overseas? Which international alumni can help you build on some of your own signature programs?

ENDNOTES

36. Lauren Thomas, email correspondence with author, June 3. 2009. Thomas, now Lauren Massy, is now the director of alumni affairs for the International School of Kuala Lumpur.

37. Jackie Tarrant-Barton, telephone interview with author, July 21, 2009.

38. Bill O'Hearn, interview with author, Eton College, Oct. 16, 2009.

39. Caralee Adams, "The Eagle Has Landed: A Little Bird Has a Big Impact in Engaging Alumni," CURRENTS 34, no. 4 (April 2008): 6–7.

40. Antonia Yeung, interview with author, Hong Kong, Nov. 6, 2009.

41. Lou Alexander, telephone interview with author, July 20, 2009.

42. Quotation from telephone interview, July 20, 2009.

43. Suda interview, June 22, 2009.

44. Marie Earle, interview with author, Vancouver, BC, July 30, 2009.

45. Oksana Carlson, telephone interview with author, Aug. 11, 2009. Carlson is now the executive director of the Global MBA and Executive MBA programs at the Johns Hopkins Carey Business School.

46. Cooke interview, Aug. 11, 2009.

CHAPTER 4

MINDING THE CASE
Forecasting for the Next Decade

What trends should be embraced?

Which practices should we hold onto?

How collaborative can your campus become?

Will international alumni relations require different types of investment?

This book began by presenting international alumni relations as a math equation: graduates plus opportunities can equal positive results. Beyond this simple description is a compelling argument to care about how international alumni are engaged.

The beginning of this book also asked whether we are willing to change the way we think of international alumni relations. Are we willing to invest in a continual learning process?

We must help ourselves and others understand the relevance of international alumni relations in light of future administrative and educational practices, demographic changes, economic trends and globalization.

The theme of collaboration runs through this book. Schools, colleges and universities are becoming more collaborative internally and externally. Within an organization, advancement staffs are working with admissions offices, academic departments and student services. A move toward more integrated planning could lead to greater efficiencies in budgeting and communications. Externally, institutions can work with peers and partners.

INSEAD's success with working with alumni abroad is attributed to a commitment by its constituents for clear and forward-looking communications and a consistency with its brand. As technology has developed over the last five to 10 years, the staff and alumni leaders have reacted with new and progressive approaches.

"One thing I definitely see changing is that we've got this great geographic model, but I don't think it's enough," says Marisa Cooke, director of alumni affairs and the INSEAD Alumni Fund.* "We need to slice and dice, particularly with young alumni who are not thinking regionally. We are seeing more interest in affinity groups and clubs such as entrepreneurship, private equity and energy, for instance. The notion of (being) without borders and interconnectivity is what we are focusing on."

Craig Mc Kenna, associate director of alumni relations and services, explains: "What we've had is a vertical list of clubs in each country and now we're turning it around. We need to go transnational. We need to be global. For example, INSEAD Alumni Energy Clubs exist in many countries. We're now breaking down boundaries. A global club and committee have been created and this network is being fed through the academic hub (Social Innovation Centre) on campus as well as through the clubs which exist on a country level. This notion is extremely important, as it is at the country association level that events are organized according to the make up and needs of the local community, yet it is the global club which is helping to shape the strategy across the world."†

With clubs such as these, INSEAD is promoting a professional, regional and global alumni affiliation. The national aspect is also important, since it provides a very credible, larger base for the local affinity group.

It is essential to house alumni clubs within the national associations. In the long run, more volunteers will be involved at an industry level and the total number of club volunteers will likely increase, ensuring an ongoing continuity for clubs and associations in each country.

*Marisa Cooke, telephone interview with author, Aug. 11, 2009.

†Craig McKenna, telephone interview with author, Aug. 11, 2009.

International alumni relations is about building unique and personal relationships with individuals who have chosen to study at your school—with your alumni. When you are "selling" your institution, remember that you are not selling cars or designer jeans. Consider options, risks and rewards carefully when choosing to program with another school, open a satellite campus or commit to a regional fundraising scheme. Decide on a few collaborative goals for the next few years, measure the effectiveness of the effort, document progress and be open to modification.

It's not too late to begin an international alumni relations program! While this book has presented many ideas and tips that can offer inspiration today, you should also keep in mind the following considerations, which will help us think proactively about these changes in the decade ahead and new opportunities to strengthen our position.

Consideration #1: Campuses need to coordinate all international engagement.

From international undergraduate recruiting schedules, to study abroad programs, to faculty sabbaticals, these points of engagement require planning, communication and collaboration. An example of a university's comprehensive system of tracking international engagement can be found at the University of Cincinnati. The UC Online System for Managing International Collaboration, or UCosmic, took four years to develop under the leadership of a vice provost for international affairs.[1] UCosmic is a database used by the university community. As information about travel schedules and the history of academic programs was added to the database, the university began to see patterns of time, resources and program longevity. Having the ability to assess international engagement in a comprehensive way also provides opportunity to make some changes, reallocate resources and better align the campus's international practices to overall mission, academic opportunities and advancement priorities. UCosmic was an instrumental piece in place before the launch of the university's capital campaign in late 2008.

Several universities around the world share this strategic direction in their leadership. Oxford University has a director of international strategy who reports to the vice-chancellor. The National University of Singapore's vice president of global relations also oversees planning and academic outreach. (Fifty percent of NUS students go abroad sometime during their four years at the university.)

At Michigan State, nearly a dozen units across the university have formed a partnership called the Forming Partnerships for International Initiatives Committee. "This forum allows the university to push through institutional barriers on international issues through the participation of a broad range of university units," says Michigan State's Claire Brender, director of international alumni relations (a position that was created in 2009).[2] Participants represent the offices of admissions, university relations, the MSU Alumni Association, university advancement, the Office of International Students and Scholars, and other units of international studies and programs.

The recent recession, however, has led some universities to cut back their international efforts by eliminating the "senior international officer" and disseminating resources in functional areas such as study abroad or as international grant applications for faculty.[3] These institutions are making the decision to decentralize the management of international affairs.

My recommendation is to establish and maintain a coordinated effort. It will be harder to catch up on "being global" if you step out instead of thinking about how to stay afloat during downturns.

Consideration #2: International advancement officers will perform multiple functions.

Along with the implementation of a campus-wide international program, schools and universities will require professional staff working abroad to wear many hats:

those of the admissions, alumni relations and development offices. Skilled, knowledgeable and entrepreneurial professionals with at least more than one major staff responsibility help keep their institution's international program operating efficiently. The breadth of resources and information available to international alumni, parents, prospective students and guidance counselors should be much more comprehensive. As mentioned previously, the University of Toronto's satellite office in Hong Kong bridges admissions, alumni relations and development functions in East Asia. Institutions that embrace hybrid roles or the idea of cross-training across functions have an opportunity to develop their employees and their international programs.

Begin cross-training with interns and new hires. A new program such as the CASE Europe–HEFCE Graduate Trainee Program provides year-long paid internships in fundraising offices of several U.K. universities.[4] Interns learn about prospect research and donor relations, and are given an opportunity to discover strategies for fundraising both domestically and internationally.

Consideration #3: Some international alumni relations program should generate revenue.

As this book has illustrated, successful international relations programs require regular attention, adequate funding and new ideas. Working with international constituents costs more money per person than when working domestically. Today's economic and demographic conditions create a license for alumni relations to begin to think about some programs as a business.

"When will international alumni relations offices become profit centers rather than cost centers?" asked Shelley Nason, senior director for alumni relations and development for Europe, Middle East and Africa for the University of Chicago.[5] Nason is based in London.

"With life expectancy for men and women increasing, we will have a sixty- to sixty-five-year window to leverage the relationship between the graduate and his/her alma mater," adds Daniel J. Guhr, principal of the Illuminate Consulting Group, an international education consultancy based outside of San Francisco.[6]

Guhr continues, "The alumni relations strategy should be central to the business strategy of higher education. We can re-educate alumni with programs which bring top faculty directly to alumni."

By following the first assumption of employing an integrated international strategy, a campus can enable the best conditions from which to plan attractive alumni programs. Modify existing programs to coincide with faculty travel or major conferences. Create opportunities to introduce new leaders to international alumni by planning regional receptions, mini-symposia, and other general initiatives designed to attract a wide range of alumni, parents and friends. These types of events are usually free and/or designed to have much of their costs underwritten.

Revenue-generating programs will become part of the alumni programming menu for more universities in the next decade. Travel-learn programs have already been turning small profits for years. These programs have offered alumni, parents and friends an exclusive opportunity to travel the world with fellow graduates and learn from faculty escorts. Through this access, travelers are given access to information (about the trip's subject matter and the institution) for a small premium.

Consider the major demographic shift for the next decade: more baby boomers are retiring, and even with our latest recession, there are opportunities to engage educated and mobile alumni in various parts of the world. A back-to-campus experience for a reduced fee and schedule can be both attractive to the alumni and profitable to the sponsor. The program needs to be facilitated professionally and personably and should draw upon available resources abroad. Decide what "premium service" means for your institution and its alumni and think about the contributions your alumni have already made. This may be very different for private and public institutions, but going through the practice of considering profit-generating programs is worthwhile and helps redefine your programming strategy. If this third assumption is correct and if it is executed well, "the acquisition cost to acquire and reacquire alumni is $0," concludes Guhr.

Consideration #4: We will maintain traditional communication methods while continuing to adapt to new technologies.

Even with the rise of social media among almost every segment of society, and alongside the growth of new technologies such as telepresence rooms, international alumni relations will continue to benefit from traditional means of communication. Globalization is producing opportunities for universities to open up campuses abroad and some governments are actively recruiting educational investment. Initial meetings between key decision-makers in these partnerships will not be conducted through a shared online calendar or on a Facebook wall. Formal communications will continue to lead parties through negotiation, and sharing meals will probably never go out of vogue. The internationalization of education requires us to adhere to tradition.

More locally, can alumni relations rely solely on social media to advertize events and communicate with alumni overseas? This answer is, probably not, as some institutions have learned from their alumni. "An overwhelming number of young alumni are asking for email more than social media (notices)," says Nathalie Walker, head of alumni relations at Cambridge University. "It may be due to the status of how they organize their lives. Email is less invasive than social media."[7]

As institutions look ahead to the coming years, decisions about what forms of communications to uphold will occur. Some methods, such as in-person meetings and telephone calls, cost more but may be valued more. It also depends on who is involved. Educational attachés and major international donors may expect a high-touch approach. Providing a balanced communications plan so that all alumni feel valued and involved with their alma mater is essentially the goal.

Consideration #5: Internationalization of higher education will produce alumni with nontraditional affinity.

With the increase of international community college graduates, more short-term international exchange programs and executive or corporate learning programs and a growing number of institutions "exporting" their campuses to other countries and continents, the opportunities for nontraditional affinities will continue to abound in the coming years. Indeed, nontraditional affinities may become the new "norm" by the year 2021.

CONCLUSION

The assumptions above are derived from dozens of interviews with international advancement peers from around the world. The best practices shared and lessons learned lead to continuous improvement in our profession. By working with integrated campus teams; by delivering excellent service and resources and cultivating new donors; by building in a revenue stream to international programs; by maintaining interpersonal authenticity in an era of interactive media; by inviting the involvement and support of new constituents; by reacting to these forecasts—and formulating some predictions on your own in the decade ahead—your international alumni relations program will move ahead and prosper.

May we continue to reflect, share and lead by example.

ENDNOTES

1. Karin Fischer, "U. of Cincinnati Builds a System to Track Its Place in the World," *Chronicle of Higher Education*, Sept. 7, 2009, *chronicle.com/article/U-of-Cincinnati-Tracks-Its/48303/*; Mitch Leventhal, interview with author, New York City, Sept. 20, 2010.

2. Claire Brender, telephone interviews with author, Sept. 21, 2009, and Nov. 4, 2009.

3. Karin Fischer, "In Economic Downturn, Colleges Eye International Education: Cut Back or Forge Ahead?" *Chronicle of Higher Education*, Aug. 29, 2010, *chronicle.com/article/In-Economic-Downturn-Colleges/124167/*.

4. "Advance(ment) Preparation: CASE Europe-HEFCE Graduate Trainee Program Boosts Fundraising Careers in the U.K.," CURRENTS 36, no. 7 (September 2010): 51.

5. Shelly Nason, telephone interview with author, July 24, 2009; Nason, interview with author, London, Sept. 23, 2009.

6. Daniel Guhr, interview with author, South San Francisco, Sept. 12, 2009.

7. Nathalie Walker, interview with author, London, Oct. 16, 2009.

Case Studies

Woodstock School

In Mussoorie, India, the Woodstock School has been educating young minds since 1854. Thirty years ago, most financial support for the school derived from admission fees. Today, advancement professionals have targeted goals, since tuition money is not enough to keep Woodstock competitive with adequate staffing, services and updates to its remote campus in the Himalayas.*

The school's development office works closely with volunteer alumni and parents to secure solid support for the school. The school is in touch with 5,500 alumni, of which 4,600 share email addresses with the school. The Woodstock Old Students' Association (WOSA), the school's umbrella alumni organization, started more than 100 years ago and serves all alumni. Anyone who attends for one semester qualifies as an alumnus. Former staff (faculty and administration) are included as full members of WOSA.

WOSA has three chartered groups: WOSA Europe, WOSA India and WOSA North America (WOSA/NA). With 3,500 alumni in the United States and Canada, the school has a vested interest in maintaining strong relations with WOSA/NA. The membership of WOSA/NA tends to be older because almost all students who left Woodstock prior to the mid-1970s went straight to college in North America. The majority of alumni in North American are over 50.

WOSA-NA has an annual reunion conference each summer that attracts between 200 and 400 alumni and guests. The traditional schedule for the conference has included workshops on modern Indian politics and culture and has featured distinguished alumni speakers who share information about their careers. Instead of getting together for fundraisers, alumni gather to talk about India today and how their graduates and families are doing around the world. There is also time for storytelling. During the opening night of the reunions, alumni talk about their era of Woodstock history.

During the reunions in the early 1990s, the topic of Third Culture Kids (TCK) was on the top of everyone's list. It was extremely important for the older alumni to realize that being a Third Culture Kid was not a unique experience but shared among most alumni at that time. WOSA/NA seized the opportunity to encourage those conversations, both at reunions and throughout the year. In today's age of mobile technology and with more students living and studying in more than one country, however, the TCK notion is not as significant to the younger alumni. Our global world has forever changed the experiences of students to transition in and out of cultures. In fact, TCK today are known as CCK (Cross-Cultural Kids). For more information about Third Culture Kids, see *tckid.com*.

WOSA/NA President Anne Lind is inspired to do more. "In North America we need to continue to sponsor regional gatherings of different kinds, especially emphasizing networking in some of the major cities."[†] Woodstock's students hail from India and more than 25 other countries. Seventy-five percent of graduating seniors go to North America for college and become international alumni during their first four years away from the Woodstock campus. The alumni relations team uses this opportunity to stay in touch with this cohort.

Lind is happy about the uses of Woodstock's electronic communications and social media. To help alumni meet each other without spending money on events, the school encourages all alumni to post their work and personal travel schedules to WOSA's online community. The alumni relations office is tracking the number of submissions posted and how alumni are using this information.

Back in Mussoorie, the alumni relations office is part of a centralized development office. The school has a director of development, two alumni relations officers, two communications officers and an office manager. Additionally, the Friends of Woodstock School (FWS) foundation in the United States has a part-time employee with long ties to the school who works to develop the base of support in North America.

In spring of 2010, a new development director started an internship program for 10 second-semester juniors and first-semester seniors. The benefits of the internship program were two-fold: 10 more part-time interns augment the staffing structure during the majority of the year; in turn, the office provides a training ground for new alumni. The professional staff has developed multiple job descriptions for the internships. Both staff and students feel the program is working well. Students like the idea of getting some "real-world" job experience to add to their college applications, and Woodstock knows it has to pay attention to the interests and needs of the youngest alumni.

Woodstock is also paying attention to the needs of their oldest or less-connected alumni. Through contact reports and conversation, Woodstock learned that a potential donor wanted to know the latest news about the school but could only rely on the annual magazine for information. She did not have an email address and had no plans to start using that method of communication. The school decided to remedy the situation by creating a student phone corps. This group of students (some of whom may be interns or trained by the interns) would schedule individual conversations with alumni around the world who wanted a "live" connection to Mussoorie, India. Promotional material in the magazine invited alumni to choose this option, if they desired. Calls could be made from the school at the right time to reach the alumni, and the international dialing plan at the school meant this effort would not be too costly. There were many benefits for maintaining the traditional phone call:

- It is a live, two-way conversation.
- There is flexibility in scheduling.
- It encourages intergenerational contact.
- It is cost-effective.
- It is personal.
- It is likely to result in some form of long-term benefit to the school.

The development and alumni relations team realizes the most effective program for the coming years is one that is flexible enough to adjust to the changing priorities, interests and needs of their alumni. Exposing current students to alumni relations is another way of increasing involvement. Expanding the ways in which the school communicates with alumni provides another avenue of engagement. The annual conference in North America is a good platform for sharing both WOSA and the school's vision with a wide range of alumni. In 2011, WOSA celebrated its centennial, and the school is mindful of the importance of maintaining important traditions while looking to the future and its alumni for inspiration and support.

*Unless otherwise noted, the information in this case study gathered by the author during her visit to Woodstock School, Nov. 4-5, 2010.

†Anne Lind, telephone interview with author, Aug. 9, 2009.

University of California at Davis

University of California at Davis is one of the 10 campuses in the University of California system. UC Davis is a comprehensive land-grant research university with four undergraduate colleges, six professional schools, and more than 80 graduate programs. More than 30,000 students are enrolled, with over 2,200 from more than 90 countries, plus over 2,500 international scholars (the fourth-highest number in the United States) from 100 countries. Nearly 200,000 living alumni are counted, but UC Davis has accurate email or physical address for fewer than 50 percent of these. Approximately 20,000 alumni live outside the United States.

UC Davis, like other University of California campuses, is autonomous; but all campuses in the University of California system report to a single Board of Regents, and the UC Davis chancellor reports to the president of the University of California.

UC Davis' strategy for an international alumni relations strategic plan began in 2001 when the position of assistant vice provost of international alumni and development was initiated. Robert A. Kerr was selected to fill this position and was given the directive to develop a new program for UC Davis.

Kerr spent his first two years at UC Davis verifying alumni records in an effort to bring as much integrity to the data as possible so that future programs and communications could reach as many alumni as possible. He and his staff accomplished this task through direct mail, email and travel (holding alumni events in many locations) and by involving faculty contacts who traveled for academic programs, sabbaticals and/or were in touch with former students living abroad. After each international event, Kerr would assess the readiness of that region to build a local UC Davis international network.

During the next two years, Kerr and his team created an additional channel of communications between UC Davis and its alumni. Kerr and others continued to export programs abroad and build relationships with its alumni. The International Programs Newsletter, featuring alumni profiles, was launched to international and campus audiences (primarily electronic with a few hard copies delivered to campus offices). International network activities coincided as much as possible with the chancellor, faculty and senior administrators' international travel schedules.

In 2005, UC Davis promoted Kerr to assistant vice provost for international alumni and development, and he continued identifying and developing International Network leaders throughout the next two years. The personal experiences of alumni and UC Davis administration and faculty during in subsequent years helped solidify future engagement and outreach. UC Davis was remaining consistent, communicative and conscientious about the needs and interest of its international constituents. More alumni were self-identifying as volunteers for UC Davis.

The university began to use social media tools more fully beginning in 2007. After building an updated database, establishing credibility and trust through regular communications and in-person visits and promoting its international networks, UC Davis used interactive web tools to attract more interest and participation in both international alumni and academic activities.

UC Davis has 30 international alumni networks in 23 countries (outside the United States) for some 184,000 alumni and scholars around the world. The "scholars" are fulfilling post-doctorate, sabbatical, UC Davis Extension certificate, Fulbright programs and other named-grant opportunities. The Cal Aggie Alumni Association (CAAA) and development office are Kerr's primary partners in the office of university relations. He has a dotted-line reporting relationship to CAAA and development executive directors.

"What makes UC Davis unique is our definition of alumni to include scholars," says Kerr.* "We are tracking our scholars with as much diligence as we are our alumni." Fifty percent of these scholars come mid-career to study at Davis.

Kerr continues, "UC Davis has built our program on friend-raising, not fundraising. We are working on long-term gains. In 2001, we didn't have good international initiatives to talk about, and now we have four!"

UC Davis' strategy for developing an international alumni relations program has been supported by several best practices:

- Facilitating communications with deans and development directors by meeting regularly to discuss who is traveling where/when, international network activity schedule, sabbatical faculty located abroad, etc.
- Communicating with international networks and leaders a minimum of seven times annually through electronic publications with a consistent brand/message of "Doing what matters" and "Building Bridges."
- Conducting a common program across all international networks: Picnic Day, an annual campus event held the third Saturday of April.
- Holding an alumni and friends event and meeting with international network leaders whenever the chancellor or other senior administrators and faculty travel abroad.
- Creating a website featuring international network leader information, most recent alumni activity and upcoming events.

UC Davis also takes steps to make sure that alumni and students interact:

- Alumni hold receptions for students studying abroad.
- Alumni provide internships at international locations.
- Alumni fund scholarships for students from abroad to study at UC Davis and for UC Davis students to study abroad.
- Alumni and scholars serve a presenters at international student fairs, which offer opportunities to recruit students.

Additionally, administration and faculty interact with alumni to ensure program support:

- Holding meetings between the chancellor and other senior staff members and UC Davis alumni and scholars who host meals and receptions.
- Providing travel arrangements and advice on local customs and culture to the advancement staff.
- Exploring research and educational collaborations, including information about foreign funding opportunities through government and private sector grants.
- Supporting the exchange of graduate students and active recruitment of UC Davis students to international graduate programs.

Finally, UC Davis has found success in its development objectives. Receiving gifts-in-kind, including the hosting of receptions and meals, discounted or free lodging, is one priority. Identifying funding for students traveling abroad (e.g., a round-trip airline ticket) is another. Together, these contributions are the first steps to identifying a major donor prospect abroad.

UC Davis and Kerr keep an eye on their annual performance by evaluating the number of contact reports, their fundraising goal, the communication connections through websites and electronic exchanges and the exposure of international alumni in campus publications and as award recipients.

Looking ahead to the coming years, Kerr is confident of UC Davis' readiness and ability to change with the realities of fluctuating financial forecasts and an aging population. He envisions that the CAAA travel program will have greater linkages. International network leader news, events invitations and campus updates will continue to be communicated through email, newsletters, websites, Facebook and Twitter.

Kerr has goals for expanding the alumni experience to include more students and families. Steps include tracking trends of locations for international students and scholars attending UC Davis, tracking the trends of locations for UC Davis students studying abroad and creating a "family" feeling while international students and scholars study at UC Davis by partnering with student affairs departments and CAAA. This step will help increase data integrity by capturing information while students and scholars are on campus.

Finally, with expanded and strengthened collaboration with campus units, Kerr and his colleagues will continue to conserve travel resources and time.

UC Davis' model is rooted in the experiences of its alumni, as former students and scholars, both on campus and abroad. Staying focused on the relationships since Day 1 has prepared the institution to confidently move forward as a leader in international outreach.

*Robert A. Kerr, telephone interview with author, July 23, 2009.

Central European University

"We were born in 1991, but the first degree was conferred in the 1993–94 academic year," says Serge Sych, director of alumni and corporate relations at Central European University in Budapest.* CEU was founded in the wake of political and social reform. The CEU website provides a succinct rendering of its founding and its mission:

Central European University was founded in 1991 with the explicit aim of helping the process of transition from dictatorship to democracy in Central and Eastern Europe and Central Asia. It was committed to bringing together students from these 30 countries and from the West in order to nurture respect for diverse cultures and opinions, human rights, constitutional government, and the rule of law. In its first decade, CEU sought to contribute to innovative academic research, progressive higher education and the development of dynamic, sustainable open society primarily in the former "socialist" countries. More recently, its interest has become global, with special attention paid to emerging democracies throughout the world. These aims—all in step with promoting the values of the Open Society—remain fundamental to CEU, but our mission has become global with special attention to emerging democracies worldwide. Nowadays, half of the applicants to CEU come from almost 100 countries of all five continents beyond its historic focus region.

While working on his law degree in 1999, Sych applied for—and got—the new position at CEU to set up an alumni relations program. Alumni relations was such a new concept to Sych that he had to check the dictionary "because I didn't know what the term *alumni* meant," he admits. Sych believes that a question from George Soros, honorary chairman of the Board of Trustees, and well-known billionaire, was "good enough to start the program." Soros apparently wanted to know where alumni of CEU were and what they were doing.

Knowing he would be accountable to Soros and others, Sych's first item of business was to build a database. He started completely from scratch. He was heading up a program that didn't exist and he was an alumnus as well. Working with the student records office, he started by using the student graduation forms and worked the phones and the Internet for updated information. He approached more than 100 universities during the first year to learn about the alumni relations profession and the types of services and support different models offered. Sych also benefitted by attending professional conferences and widening his professional network.

The CEU in-house alumni database was established in three years. CEU's 1,540 students represent more than 100 countries. The majority are from Central Europe and the independent states of the former Soviet Union. Including its business school, CEU has 8,500 alumni, and 90 percent of these are addressable. Within four years of starting the alumni relations program, Sych hired another staff member. Today, three staff members work with the program. There is limited opportunity for staff to travel outside of Budapest for alumni events.

CEU's 40 to 50 chapters, ranging from five to 400 alumni, provide coverage to almost the entire alumni constituency. Even with larger groups in Moscow, Kiev, Budapest, London and New York City, the chapters are very informal and do not have any organizational guidelines to date. Since 2001, CEU hosts an annual alumni assembly meeting in Budapest. Some chapter leaders apply for travel stipends. The alumni association was formed in 2002.

The alumni relations program at CEU is integrated with the career programming office and, in turn, the involvement of international alumni with the student recruitment process. "Fifty percent of our admitted students were referred to CEU by alumni," states Sych. He works closely with alumni to help them identify students and to serve as resources during the application process. "Alumni see this as the most important role they can play," he continues.

Beyond recruiting students, alumni have played another important role in the recent past. In 2007, administrative and budget cuts at CEU forced Sych to think about the strongest alliances for the alumni relations program. These were the alumni who could help as mentors and resources to the students. Starting that fall, new students were introduced to alumni during orientation week. Students heard themselves called "alumni-in-training" during these first weeks on campus.

For CEU, therefore, their best practices start with interaction between the students and their alumni. Sych and his staff enjoy working with their alumni groups on a program that they like and want to do, and they believe that student recruitment is a way for alumni to get involved. There is a visible synergy of working with career programs as alumni resources are directly delivered to students, offering a valuable service at an early point in the student's career. Building community among a culturally diverse alumni body is also a goal.

"It's all about people," Sych says. "One or two individuals can energize others. They are so young and starting families and in jobs … it's hard to get volunteer commitment—even more so than the financial commitment."

Sych and his staff annually evaluate their efforts and outline performance planning goals for the coming year. To date, most of their goals have centered on participation numbers in alumni programs and on how many students were recruited to CEU. As CEU is still young, the average age of a CEU alumnus is just 35 years. Current benchmarking practices, therefore, do not include how much money they raise from alumni; rather, they measure how many students' tuition dollars are generated from the efforts of their alumni recruiters.

Sych and CEU believe they have found the right engagement model for the next five years. The professional and career development focus and a network of internationally placed alumni will afford students and alumni meaningful interaction. CEU also predicts it will attract more corporate partners as companies fulfill their corporate responsibility mission by linking their human resources offices to the career services offices and related alumni networks. In the end, the model will pay off, however slowly. "We will also have an increased demand for financial donation, but we have a long way to go to increase this," says Sych.

Sych is an enduring and positive presence at the university. "I always say to my staff we're forced to try many things on our own. We're tailor-made and have fit a program to the alumni needs of today." With more than 100 countries and cultures involved, there is no one-size solution to the CEU program. "We're flexible. We don't have traditions, and the freedom is challenging," concludes Sych.

*Serge Sych, telephone interview with author, June 25, 2009.

University of British Columbia

"Global Citizenship" is the theme of the University of British Columbia's institutional vision. About 15 percent of its current undergraduate population is international; that number rises to 30 percent for its graduate-level students. More than 3,000 of its 260,000 alumni live in Hong Kong.

We spoke with Catherine Folk, president of the UBC Alumni Association in Hong Kong, for a closer look at what drives a dedicated alumni volunteer. Our telephone conversation took place Oct. 18, 2010.

Gretchen Dobson: Why are you involved?

Catherine Folk: I always have a tie to UBC, but the main reasons are that I met my husband [there] and my older daughter graduated from UBC and my younger daughter is a student there today. When we talk about UBC there are a lot of fun things to remember. My years there were one of the happiest moments of my life.

I joined the alumni association a long time ago but was more active in 2006. UBC gave me a platform from which to contribute to the community.

GD: As the association president, how do you attract volunteers?

CF: When I started we had a similar objective on the community concern team (formerly called the charity committee). We worked together and had a common goal. We didn't have any direction, but we knew we wanted to contribute to the community. We raised funds and had the chance to contribute back to the community.

Today, there are a lot of human relationships to sort out. We just had our annual General Meeting, and as president, I'm now in the process of recruiting new executive board members. I have about 31 members who are registered and want to be part of these teams:

- Community Concern team
- Social team
- Professional Development team
- Alumni Association Development team – PR and Membership

The structure has been there for about three years but I have restructured it a bit. Some advice: name the committees something a little more exciting than "administrative."

GD: For the Membership team, your executive members are responsible for welcoming new members through at least two events. How often are events held?

CF: During the last year, we had at least two events from each team each month. For example in August, we had a Green Trip from the Community Concern team and a bowling trip. We do not charge dues and everyone pays for events.

GD: What are you most passionate about?

CF: I am most passionate about one of our most popular programs. I was most involved in the Community Concern team. We wanted to do something meaningful so we aligned with another association that visited elderly in their homes. In the Chinese culture we have the mid-Autumn festival, which represents families coming together. Our last was on September 15, 2010. We delivered moon cakes to residents and visited elderly in their home (most are by themselves). Fifty percent of the elderly live in government housing. It's like an estate with 10 to 15 buildings with 30 floors, and each floor has 20 units and each unit is 360 square feet. Because it's so crowded we try to get enough alumni volunteers to see the elderly in their units.

We raise funds to do this. We have a walkathon to raise funds. Our alumni association buys moon cakes, fruits, and contributes other items to goody bags. We have been participating in this activity for the last three years and will plan on doing so in 2011.

This year we went to a more remote housing section in the New Territories and we had about 30 volunteers. Alumni bring their family members.

Our other objective was to test their alarms in their homes. The residents have alert buttons in their homes, but we felt it important to survey their physical conditions. The alumni are learning how to relate to elderly folks.

This year we were nominated as a "Caring Organization" by the Hong Kong Government. We were not elected because we do not have a staff, but we could be nominated for volunteering enough hours.

GD: Do you have a wish list item from the UBC Central Office in Vancouver?

CF: Yes, I can think of a couple of things.

First, it would be great if the alumni association in Hong Kong had a small amount of money to add to their account. We raise funds on our own and participants pay for all their events.

Also, it would help if some funding would be available to the Professional Development team so we could secure more centrally located venues for our events.

I also have a new idea for this year. We want to have a reunion in Hong Kong on a day that all the teams will do one activity together. It would be the first time area alumni could come together for one main event.

GD: The president's term is one year. Would you run again?

CF: I have to find someone to replace me in the future. I am a graduate of 1979, and those who are joining are from a younger crowd. My hope is not to run, but my job is to find the right person to take over. The alumni association has grown so much and so fast that it's becoming a big job. The more structured it is, the more work we create.

University of California, Berkeley, Haas School of Business

Historically, the University of California, Berkeley, has played a prominent role in country-building through its education of young leaders from throughout the world. As part of the International House movement in the early 20th century and in recognition of its large population of foreign students, UC Berkeley was chosen in 1930 as the site for the second U.S. "I-House," a dormitory for students from around the world. The I-House fosters relationships between international students and is noted for having been home to many famous leaders.

UC Berkeley has especially strong and long-standing ties with Asia, going back more than a century. In 2010, the university was ranked No. 2 in Shanghai Jiao Tong University's Academic Ranking of World Universities.

Each entering class of 240 in the UC Berkeley Haas Business School's full-time MBA program comprises, on average, close to 40 percent international students. As the students from abroad have increased, so too, have the program demands for alumni relations and recruiting for those with international interests.

Business graduates understand the value of networking. In Shanghai, graduates of about 20 MBA programs from different foreign business schools have formed a network, and the Berkeley-Haas alumni chapter in Shanghai is a member.

The numbers of Chinese alumni of foreign business schools living in China is growing. Because the recent financial turmoil has made it more difficult to be hired in the United States, many of newly minted MBA holders are returning to China—and are being joined by expats coming to take advantage of growing economic opportunities there. Do growing alumni numbers lead to more donations?

Ann Hsu, who was a driving force behind the establishment of the Berkeley-Haas alumni chapter in Shanghai (see sidebar), understands that, for an alumni organization, fundraising is a priority, but it will take some time to realize an overall increase in participation. "With the relatively young age of alumni in China, the alumni staying here are not as advanced in their careers and they don't have a lot to donate. They do understand what philanthropy is: doing things for others and donating money," says Hsu. "If the goal is to raise money in the coming five to 10 years, this is not realistic, since we have a young alumni base. We can plant the idea, though. Even if they hit it big, they are less likely to donate as compared to an alumnus in Silicon Valley."*

In other words, if business schools (and other institutions) cultivate alumni organizations in China throughout this decade, they create a much greater chance of fundraising after 2020. As alumni mature and enter their 40s, they may be more inclined to give back to alma mater.

Jeanne Huang Li, senior director of development at Berkeley-Haas who handles international outreach and development, reports that ultimately, effective engagement and cultivation of overseas alumni involve development of an awareness of the region—starting on campus. Berkeley has historically had strong Asian studies programs. In other activities of the school specific to Asia, the Berkeley-Haas School of Business launched its Asia Business Center (ABC) in 2008. According to Asia Business Center website, "The ABC develops high-impact programs and forges strategic partnerships between University of California, Berkeley and reputable institutions in Asia to provide excellence and leadership in management education and research."[†]

In the fall of 2010, the ABC inaugurated a Fellows program, offering promising business leaders and scholars from China an opportunity to study at Haas. These visiting scholars will also be welcomed as alumni to further increase the network.

In March 2011, Berkeley-Haas, through its Asia Business Center, conducted a highly successful conference in Shanghai. With the vice mayor of Shanghai as a guest of honor, keynote speakers and special guests included its 2009 Nobel Prize Winner in Economics, the CEO of Novartis, the dean and prominent professors. The event was well attended by Chinese nationals and partners as well as alumni. Ann Hsu, the Shanghai alumni chapter and alumni from throughout Asia played a crucial role in making the conference a success.

Students from Berkeley-Haas have shown tremendous interest in China, with over a third of the first-year MBA class traveling to China as part of a student study trek in January 2010. Students at Berkeley-Haas also organize highly successful annual Asia business conferences on campus; the 11th annual was held April 2, 2011. The school also offers regular study treks, project teams through the school's international business development program, and seminars in international business to Asia.

To balance the focus on Asia, the dean of Berkeley-Haas has also made successful trips to Latin America and Europe recently, and the school is happy to report active alumni chapters and activities throughout the world.

[*]Ann Hsu, telephone interview with author, July 28, 2010.

[†]*asiabusiness.haas.berkeley.edu/.*

ANN HSU

Meet Ann Hsu, a 1998 MBA graduate of the University of California, Berkeley, Haas School of Business. She is married, has two children, and works in the Internet industry. A Shanghai native, Hsu returned to China in 2006, and one of the first steps she took when she got to Shanghai was to send an email to the Berkeley-Haas online alumni community, letting her fellow alumni know she was organizing an event. This first event attracted 14 alumni. For the next two years, once a quarter, Hsu would organize informal social alumni events. In 2008, when the dean of

Berkeley-Haas and a contingent from the school visited Shanghai, Hsu met Leslie Kanberg, director of alumni relations for Berkeley-Haas. Kanberg and Hsu discussed forming an alumni chapter. "Maybe it wouldn't be much more work than before," Hsu thought at the time.*

Hsu's willingness to invest her own time in the process was key, but so too was the readiness of others in the community. Alumni wanted to build professional and personal support networks. "[I thought] maybe other expats would also seek a network outside of work, especially those with a family. When you arrive, it is helpful to find other people who have similar backgrounds. Haas School is a common connection we can trust," explains Hsu.

Kanberg and her colleagues back in Berkeley were also ready to support a new alumni group, but what were Hsu's next steps? To initiate the chapter, Hsu personally called her contacts to form a board. Her goal was to bring together a diverse group of alumni: single, married, expats and some native Chinese.

The first project sponsored by the board was an alumni survey distributed by email. Additionally, at events over a three- to four-month period, alumni were asked to complete surveys. "We found that others preferred to have informal, standing events once a month, and one to two times a year they would like to have a bigger event, such as hosting the dean or bringing in a professional speaker. [But] probably no more than once or twice a year for the larger events, because people are busy," Hsu cautions.

A family friendly event was dubbed Mega Play Date (MPD). In order to foster a sense of family between fellow alumni and to encourage those with families to involve their families, the chapter organized a day at a resort where both adults and children were entertained. Activities included swimming, gym access and enough adult and child time programmed in to please everyone. The second and even more successful MPD was held in July 4, 2010, and the tradition continued in 2011.

International alumni are transient, and that may have an impact on the sustainability of a group. Hsu agrees but is not dissuaded by change and remains pragmatic: "In the last four months, I had three board members who moved out of town. This takes some of the momentum away, but on the other hand, it affords an opportunity for others to get involved. We have a few new alumni in town, so I will involve them. To me, this is not a high pressure thing. I don't feel I need to answer to anybody. I'm not getting paid. It's a personal thing and I won't pressure anyone to participate."

But more alumni want to at least affiliate with Berkeley-Haas in China.

"I think some new alumni are looking for professional connections, and our name is known [in Shanghai]," says Hsu. "Alumni will look us up and quickly connect. Even students connect when they are on summer jobs. Some come on vacation time to check out opportunities.

"I feel like we are family. We are here if you need us. We don't force anything, but are here as a resource."

Because of the excellent efforts of Ann Hsu and her amazing team of fellow alumni volunteers in Shanghai, the chapter was named the Alumni Chapter of the Year in 2009. Hsu is a member of the Dean's Advisory Circle.

*Information and quotations in this sidebar from Ann Hsu, telephone interview with author, July 28, 2010, and email correspondence with author, Aug. 1, 2011.

University of Phoenix

The University of Phoenix is not your traditional university. It's the largest private university in the United States, boasting more than 600,000 alumni in over 130 countries. More than 400,000 students study at over 200 campus locations and through online programs.

The University of Phoenix does not fundraise, and the alumni association does not charge dues. Until a few years ago, most University of Phoenix students were studying for graduate degrees; today, the institution has more new and transfer students choosing to fulfill their associate and bachelor degrees, and Phoenix has been building an alumni program to serve the needs and interests of the overall growing number of alumni.

Adrienne Marcus, the alumni association's senior manager of operations, says that Phoenix does not have an international alumni relations number to report, since international alumni are not counted separately. "We treat all alumni the same and offer the same resources to all. If there is a campus present, we want them to engage at the campus level."*

Phoenix has a campus in Puerto Rico, and it may look more like your campus than you'd think. Founded in 1980, the campus offers associate, bachelor, master's, and doctorate degrees. The theme for their third annual Homecoming, in 2010, was "Networking for Success."

The European campus is located in Germany near the Ramstein Air Base, and more than 300 MBA alumni live in Rotterdam and surrounding area. Phoenix appeals to military personnel, since students can easily transport the online educational program as they are stationed in various parts of the world. This benefit transfers to military spouses as well.

In the *Phoenix Focus,* the alumni association's monthly online magazine, alumni profiles provide a way for graduates to stay connected to the expanding web of alumni around the world. As of December 2010, the magazine had 51,000 alumni subscribers from more than 60 countries.

Another service that operates online and has no geographical boundaries is the alumni mentor program. Alumni from associate to doctoral programs are matched by degree level and academic specialization. "If an alumnus from the U.S. wants to meet the ballet director in the Philippines, we can do that," says Alanna Vitucci, executive director of alumni relations.[†] Launched in 2009, the program now includes 30,000 registered alumni who are available to mentor or be mentored. By the end of 2010, more than 3,200 alumni matches had been made.

Vitucci and her team disseminate an annual alumni survey. Responses can be isolated by country and region. Results from the 2009 survey show an increased interest in "connecting virtually." Recently, international alumni formed a subgroup in the alumni association's LinkedIn group.

From traditional programs such as Homecoming and career panels to creating more online connections and community, the University of Phoenix has quickly made a difference in the lives of its alumni. Vitucci and her team will be placing more emphasis on their global community. "My hope is to make what is U.S.-centric translate internationally," affirms Vitucci.

For more information, see a*lumni.phoenix.edu/.*

*Adrienne Marcus, telephone interview with author, Dec. 8, 2010.

†Alanna Vitucci, telephone interview with author, Dec. 21, 2010.

Related Resources

GENERAL

Adams, Caralee. "The Eagle Has Landed: A Little Bird Has a Big Impact in Engaging Alumni."
CURRENTS 34, no. 4 (April 2008): 6–7.
*www.case.org/Publications_and_Products/CURRENTS/CURRENTS_Archive/2008/
April_2008/Advance_Work_The_Eagle_Has_Landed.html.*

Alexander, Louis. "Network Views: University Holds Events by Alumni for Alumni."
CURRENTS 36, no. 3 (March 2010): 39–41.
*www.case.org/Publications_and_Products/CURRENTS/CURRENTS_Archive/2010/
March_2010/Network_Views.html.*

Banks, Melissa. "Outcomes for Alumni." In Outcomes and Impacts of International Education:
From International Student to Australian Graduate, the Journey of a Lifetime, 49–61.
Melbourne, Australia: IDP Education Pty, 2008.
*www.idp.com/PDF/Outcomes%20and%20Impacts%20of%20International%20
Education%20-%20From%20International%20Student%20to%20Australian%20
Graduate.pdf.*

Basinger, Julianne. "More U.S. Colleges Court Their Foreign Alumni." *Chronicle of Higher Education*
(April 23, 1999): A49.
chronicle.com/article/More-US-Colleges-Court-Their/26984.

Bennett, Gayle. "The Power of Two: Norwegian University Produces Separate Magazine for
International Alumni." CURRENTS 36, no. 9 (November/December 2010): 6–7.
*www.case.org/Publications_and_Products/CURRENTS/CURRENTS_Archive/2010/
NovemberDecember_2010/The_Power_of_Two.html.*

Brennan, Timothy P. "High-Tech Ties That Bind: Technology Tips for Reaching International
Alumni." CURRENTS 25, no. 9 (October 1999): 13–14.
*www.case.org/Publications_and_Products/CURRENTS/CURRENTS_Archive/1999/
October_1999/Tech_Support_High-Tech_Ties_that_Bind.html.*

Burdenski, Robert A. "Reunion Giving's Je Ne Sais Quoi: INSEAD Creates a Reunion Culture." In *More Innovations in Annual Giving: Ten Global Departures That Worked*, 23–34. Washington, DC: CASE, 2009.

Clift, Kate. "Long-Distance Connection: International School Alumni Programs Bridge Continents to Build Global Networks." CURRENTS 36, no. 7 (September 2010): 34–38. *www.case.org/Publications_and_Products/CURRENTS/CURRENTS_Archive/2010/ September_2010/Long-Distance_Connection.html.*

Connor, Michael C. "Earning the Right to Ask: Set the Scene for International Philanthropy by Making Your Constituents Feel Welcome Worldwide." CURRENTS 25, no. 9 (October 1999): 36–41. *www.case.org/Publications_and_Products/CURRENTS/CURRENTS_Archive/1999/ October_1999/Earning_the_Right_to_Ask.html.*

Cuthbert, Denise, Wendy Smith, and Janice Boey. "What Do We Really Know About the Outcomes of Australian International Education? A Critical Review and Prospectus for Future Research." *Journal of Studies in International Education* 12, no. 3 (Fall 2008): 255–75.

Danver, Patricia. "One Craft, Different Cultures: Alumni Relations Evolves to Meet Global Challenges." CURRENTS 31, no. 2 (February 2005): 16–21. *www.case.org/Publications_and_Products/CURRENTS/CURRENTS_Archive/2005/ February_2005/One_Craft_Different_Cultures.html.*

Dessoff, Alan. "Through Space and Time: Keep Far-Flung Alumni in the Institutional Folds." CURRENTS 34, no. 1 (January 2008): 26–30. *www.case.org/Publications_and_Products/CURRENTS/CURRENTS_Archive/2008/ January_2008/Through_Space_and_Time.html.*

Dobson, Gretchen. "Programming Internationally." *In Alumni Relations: A Newcomer's Guide to Success*, 2nd ed., 257–67. Washington, DC: CASE, 2010.

Duge, Edna. "International Alumni Groups." *Overseas* (December 1963): 9–11.

El Senoussi, Veronica. "The UCLA Foreign Alumni Study, 1945–70." EdD diss., University of California, Los Angeles, 1973.

"Experts Share Advice on Adding Value to International Alumni Networks." *BriefCASE* 9, no. 4 (April 2011). *www.case.org/publications_and_products/briefcase/briefcase_2011/april_2011/research_ and_news_of_note.html#Article8.*

Fitzgerald, Nancy. "All Roads Lead Back to Alma Mater: How Campuses Stay Connected with Alumni Around the Globe." CURRENTS 25, no. 9 (October 1999): 30–35.
www.case.org/Publications_and_Products/CURRENTS/CURRENTS_Archive/1999/ October_1999/All_Roads_Lead_Back_to_Alma_Mater.html.

Gairing, Wolfgang. "The Role of a National Agency." In *International Alumni Relations*, EAIE Occasional Paper no. 13, ed. David Richardson, 25–32. Amsterdam: European Association for International Education, 2001.
www.eaie.org/INTAL/wolfgang.pdf.

"Getting Started—Key Questions for International Alumni Officers." European Association for International Education.
www.eaie.org/INTAL/news.asp.

Goetzl, Sylvia, and Jill Stritter, eds. *Foreign Alumni: Overseas Links for U.S. Institutions: A Report on an AID/NAFSA Survey in 1977.* Washington, DC: National Association for Foreign Student Affairs, 1980.

Guhr, Daniel J. *Four Drivers for Alumni Networks: Mutual Advantage, Life-Long Networking, Internationalization, and Professionalization.* Belmont, CA: Illuminate Consulting Group, 2006.
www.eaie.org/INTAL/paper2006.pdf.

Hummerstone, Robert G. "World-Class Annual Funds: Here's How to Take Your Appeal Abroad to Tap Some of Your Best Prospects." CURRENTS 24, no. 4 (April 1998): 40–45.
www.case.org/Publications_and_Products/CURRENTS/CURRENTS_Archive/1998/ April_1998/World-Class_Annual_Funds.html.

Illuminate Consulting Group. *New Zealand Alumni Survey: Experiences, Attitudes and Engagement.* Wellington: New Zealand Ministry of Education, 2009.
www.educationcounts.govt.nz/publications/international/58121/1.

Kerr, Robert A. "Successful Planning for International Clubs." In *Alumni Clubs and Chapters*, ed. John A. Feudo and Paul J. Clifford, 73–81. Washington, DC: CASE, 2002.

La Moreaux, Bunnie. "Research on Follow-Up Programs for International Alumni." PhD diss., University of Alabama, 1976.

A Manual of International Alumni Relations. Washington, DC: American Alumni Council/ American College Public Relations Association, 1974.

McMurtrie, Beth. "For Tufts, the World Is a Matter of Connections: The University Builds a Global Network of Alumni to Strengthen Its International Presence." *Chronicle of Higher Education* (June 4, 2009).
chronicle.com/article/For-Tufts-the-World-Is-a/44437/.

————. "Innovators in Internationalization: Tufts University." *Chronicle of Higher Education* (June 11, 2009).
  chronicle.com/article/Innovators-in/48153/.

McNamara, Lynne A. "International Advancement: The Alumni Constituency." *CASE International Journal of Educational Advancement* 2, no. 1 (June 2001): 37–51.

McNamara, Lynne Ann McCann. "Communication Used in Institutional Advancement Efforts with International Alumni from United States Institutions of Higher Education." PhD diss., Southern Illinois University, 1998.

Mijatovic, Bojan. "The University of Zagreb and Its Alumni: A Case Study," in *International Alumni Relations,* EAIE Occasional Paper no. 13, ed. David Richardson, 3–7. Amsterdam: European Association for International Education, 2001.

Moore, Forrest. "Research Report: What Our Foreign Alumni Want." *Alma Mater: Journal of the American Alumni Council* 31, no. 5 (November 1964): 23–24.

Moore, Forrest G., and Robert E. Forman. *The University and Its Foreign Alumni: Maintaining Overseas Contacts.* Minneapolis: University of Minnesota Press, 1964.

Myrinx, Elaina M. "On Target: How Targeted Communication Helps Carnegie-Mellon Organize an International Club Network." CURRENTS 11, no. 2 (February 1985): 25.

Pulley, John. "Continental Drift: International Students Become International Alumni and Create International Institutions." CURRENTS 35, no. 9 (November/December 2009): 18–24.
  www.case.org/Publications_and_Products/CURRENTS/CURRENTS_Archive/2009/NovemberDecember_2009/Continental_Drift.html.

Read, Lillian S. "Challenges of Creating and Maintaining International Alumni Relations Programs." Master's thesis, Oregon State University, 2009.
  scholarsarchive.library.oregonstate.edu/jspui/bitstream/1957/11852/1/Read_Thesis.pdf.

Richardson, David. "Fund-Raising." In *International Alumni Relations,* EAIE Occasional Paper no. 13, ed. David Richardson, 33–39. Amsterdam: European Association for International Education, 2001.

————. "Introduction." In *International Alumni Relations,* EAIE Occasional Paper no. 13, ed. David Richardson, 1–2. Amsterdam: European Association for International Education, 2001.

Rogers, Kenneth A. "Alumni Networking." In *Professional Integration: A Guide for Students from the Developing World,* 5–24. Washington, DC: National Association for Foreign Student Affairs, 1983.
  pdf.usaid.gov/pdf_docs/PNAAV557.pdf.

Rubin, Kyna. "The Time Is Ripe: Cultivating Ties with Foreign Alumni." *International Educator* (Fall 1995): 19–23.

Rubley, Julie Nicklin. "Distance, Shmistance: Australian University Keeps Its North American Alumni Close." CURRENTS 34, no. 5 (May/June 2008): 6–7. *www.case.org/Publications_and_Products/CURRENTS/CURRENTS_Archive/2008/ MayJune_2008/Advance_Work_Distance_Shmistance.html.*

———. "International Incident: Carleton University Realized That Keeping Alumni Happy Trumps Postage Costs." CURRENTS 32, no. 5 (May/June 2006): 6. *www.case.org/Publications_and_Products/CURRENTS/CURRENTS_Archive/2006/ MayJune_2006/Advance_Work_International_Incident.html.*

"Running an International Alumni Program: Strategic Approach Works Best." BriefCASE 6, no. 11 (November 2008). *www.case.org/Publications_and_Products/BriefCASE/BriefCASE_2008/November_2008/ Research_and_News_of_Note.html#Article2.*

Salopek, Jennifer. "Sending Signals: Open University Takes Its Brand of Distance Education Global." CURRENTS 28, no. 8 (October 2001): 35–39. *www.case.org/Publications_and_Products/CURRENTS/CURRENTS_Archive/2001/ October_2001/Sending_Signals.html.*

Sidhu, Luna. "Internationalizing the Annual Fund." In *Across Frontiers: New International Perspectives on Educational Fundraising,* ed. John Mc Loughlin and Jane Joo Park, 61–72. Washington, DC: CASE, 2010.

Sigue, Jocelyn. "Postcard from Beijing: Phelps and Co. Weren't the Only Ones Going for Gold in China." CURRENTS 34, no. 9 (October 2008): 13–14. *www.case.org/Publications_and_Products/CURRENTS/CURRENTS_Archive/2008/ October_2008/Postcard_from_Beijing.html.*

Simpson, Reggie. "Global Alumni Relations: A US/UK Perspective." In *Handbook of Institutional Advancement,* 3rd ed., ed. Peter McE. Buchanan, 277–79. Washington, DC: CASE, 2000.

Stevens, Thomas Carl. "The Construction of a Questionnaire for International Alumni Follow-Up." EdD diss., Indiana University, 1963.

Trimarco, Paola. "Taking on the World: International Alumni Programming Needn't Be a Daunting Task." CURRENTS 20, no. 8 (September 1994): 32–37.

VandenBerg, Patricia. "Global Greetings: Technology Invites an Institution's Extended Family to Campus Events," CURRENTS 37, no. 4 (April 2011): 44–47. *www.case.org/Publications_and_Products/CURRENTS/CURRENTS_Archive/2011/ April_2011/Global_Greetings.html.*

Visser, Leneke. "Utrecht University's International Alumni Programme." In *International Alumni Relations,* EAIE Occasional Paper no. 13, ed. David Richardson, 15–23. Amsterdam: European Association for International Education, 2001.

Walker, Nathalie. "Tending the Flock: What to Consider When Starting an International Alumni Program." CURRENTS 37, no. 3 (March 2011): 38–41. *www.case.org/Publications_and_Products/CURRENTS/CURRENTS_Archive/2011/ March_2011/Tending_the_Flock.html.*

Walker, Theresa. "International Connection: Expatriate Alumni Enrich the Student Experience Abroad." CURRENTS 33, no. 4 (April 2007): 7. *www.case.org/Publications_and_Products/CURRENTS/CURRENTS_Archive/2007/ April_2007/Advance_Work_International_Connection.html.*

———. "Something in Common: International Schools Join Forces to Bring Alma Mater to Alumni." CURRENTS 33, no. 6 (July/August 2007): 6–7. *www.case.org/Publications_and_Products/CURRENTS/CURRENTS_Archive/2007/ JulyAugust_2007/Advance_Work_Something_in_Common.html.*

Wasch, William. "International Alumni Program—A Case Study." *Techniques* (April 1975): 19–20.

Wichlac, Jerry. "Thirty-Seven Program Ideas for Foreign Alumni." Techniques (October 1974): 10–11.

Wichlac, Jerry, and Alan Reich. "Proposition: International Alumni Deserve Attention." *Alma Mater: Journal of the American Alumni Council* 54, no. 2 (Spring 1974): 8–11.

Wulk, Jerry Ernst. "USC Foreign Alumni Association" *Exchange* (Spring 1978).

ALUMNI BENCHMARKING

Brant, Keith E., and Patrick J. Regan. "The Spectrum of Alumni Involvement: Finding Ways to Measure the Variety and Intensity of Connections with Graduates." CURRENTS 28, no. 2 (February 2002): 22–28. *www.case.org/Publications_and_Products/CURRENTS/CURRENTS_Archive/2002/ February_2002/The_Spectrum_of_Alumni_Involvement.html.*

Junker, Lenore. "Room for Improvement: Golden Gate University Has Made the Alumni Experience Better for Everyone Involved." CURRENTS 32, no. 5 (May/June 2006): 22–26. *www.case.org/Publications_and_Products/CURRENTS/CURRENTS_Archive/2006/ MayJune_2006/Room_for_Improvement.html.*

Kale, Kathryn, and Adrienne A. Rulnick. "Benchmarking in Alumni Relations." In *Alumni Relations: A Newcomer's Guide to Success,* 2nd ed., ed. John A. Feudo, 295–303. Washington, DC: CASE, 2010.

McDiarmid, Daniel C. *Improving the Effectiveness of Fundraising and Alumni Programs using International Benchmarks.* Brisbane, Australia: Centre of Philanthropy and Nonprofit Studies, Queensland University of Technology, 2006. *eprints.qut.edu.au/5985/1/5985.pdf.*

Redder, Kelly. "Easy as Pie: Communities of Practice Help Alumni Professionals Measure Results and Get the Job Done." CURRENTS 33, no. 9 (October 2007): 46–49. *www.case.org/Publications_and_Products/CURRENTS/CURRENTS_Archive/2007/October_2007/Easy_as_Pie.html.*

Saul, Jason. *Benchmarking for Nonprofits: How to Measure, Manage, and Improve Performance.* St. Paul, MN: Amherst H. Wilder Foundation, 2004.

Scully, Maura King. "Are We There Yet? Alumni Professionals Have Made Strides in Proving the Value of Their Work." CURRENTS 36, no. 1 (January 2010): 16–21. *www.case.org/Publications_and_Products/CURRENTS/CURRENTS_Archive/2010/January_2010/Are_We_There_Yet.html.*

ALUMNI COMMUNICATIONS

Amos, Ralph. "Communicating Effectively with Your Alumni." In *Alumni Relations: A Newcomer's Guide to Success,* 2nd ed., ed. John A. Feudo: 107–11. Washington, DC: CASE, 2010.

Bennett, Gayle. "Standing Out in a Crowd: UC San Diego Solicits Alumni Feedback in New Online Forum." CURRENTS 35, no. 6 (July/August 2009): 8. *www.case.org/Publications_and_Products/CURRENTS/CURRENTS_Archive/2009/JulyAugust_2009/Advance_Work_Standing_Out_in_a_Crowd.html.*

Kramer, Sean, and Rob Shoss. "Virtually Yours: Technology Offers Alumni Professionals a New Prism through Which to View Events." CURRENTS 36, no. 5 (May/June 2010): 22–25. *www.case.org/Publications_and_Products/CURRENTS/CURRENTS_Archive/2010/MayJune_2010/Virtually_Yours.html.*

McAlexander, James H., Harold F. Koenig, and John W. Schouten. "Building Relationships of Brand Community in Higher Education: A Strategic Framework for University Advancement." *CASE International Journal of Educational Advancement* 6, no. 2 (February 2006): 107–18. *www.palgrave-journals.com/ijea/journal/v6/n2/pdf/2150015a.pdf.*

Melichar, Charles. "Inside the Box: Balancing creativity with Strategy." CURRENTS 36, no. 2 (February 2010): 11–12. *www.case.org/Publications_and_Products/CURRENTS/CURRENTS_Archive/2010/February_2010/Office_Space_Inside_the_Box.html.*

Rubley, Julie Nicklin. "Conformity at Its Best: Application Makes Creating an Alumni Group Web Site a Snap." CURRENTS 34, no. 2 (February 2008): 7. *www.case.org/Publications_and_Products/CURRENTS/CURRENTS_Archive/2008/ February_2008/Advance_Work_Conformity_at_Its_Best.html.*

Thompson, Chris. "Brave Net World: CASE Survey Highlights How Online Social Communities Are Being Used in Alumni Relations." CURRENTS 35, no. 1 (January 2009): 22–26. *www.case.org/Publications_and_Products/CURRENTS/CURRENTS_Archive/2009/ January_2009/Brave_Net_World.html.*

ALUMNI SURVEYS

Borden, Victor M. H. "Using Alumni Research to Align Program Improvement with Institutional Accountability." In "Enhancing Alumni Research: European and American Perspectives," ed. David J. Weerts and Javier Vidal. Special issue, *New Directions for Institutional Research*, no. 126 (Summer 2005): 61–72.

Cabrera, Alberto F., David J. Weerts, and Bradford J. Zulick. "Making an Impact with Alumni Surveys." In "Enhancing Alumni Research: European and American Perspectives," ed. David J. Weerts and Javier Vidal. Special issue, *New Directions for Institutional Research*, no. 126 (Summer 2005): 5–17. *www.education.umd.edu/EDPL/faculty/cabrera/ CabreraWeertsZulickMakingAnImpactWithAlumniSurveys.pdf.*

Coolman, Jason. "The Science Behind Alumni Engagement: The University of Waterloo Is Crunching its Alumni Data." CURRENTS 37, no. 4 (April 2011): 36–42. *www.case.org/Publications_and_Products/CURRENTS/CURRENTS_Archive/2011/ April_2011/The_Science_Behind_Alumni_Engagement.html.*

MacDonell, Kevin. "Survey says … beware, beware!" *CoolData* (blog), Nov. 18, 2010. *cooldata.wordpress.com/2010/11/18/survey-says-beware-beware/.*

Pearson, Jerold. "Become a Survey Sophisticate: Learn How to Tweak Alumni Surveys to Increase Response Rates." CURRENTS 37, no. 5 (May/June 2011): 20–23. *www.case.org/Publications_and_Products/CURRENTS/CURRENTS_Archive/2011/ MayJune_2011/Become_a_Survey_Sophisticate.html.*

Peterson, Erin. "Know Your Market: Solid Market Research Can Improve Alumni Outreach Efforts." CURRENTS 34, no. 9 (October 2008): 26–31. *www.case.org/Publications_and_Products/CURRENTS/CURRENTS_Archive/2008/ October_2008/Know_Your_Market.html.*

Shoss, Rob. "Conversation Piece: Alumni Surveys Provide Helpful Data—and Encourage Communication Between Alumni and Alma Mater." CURRENTS 31, no. 3 (March 2005): 54–57.
www.case.org/Publications_and_Products/CURRENTS/CURRENTS_Archive/2005/March_2005/Conversation_Piece.html.

van Nostrand, Innes. "A Picture of Health: Emerging Research Trends Can Give You a Better Understanding of Your Alumni Body." CURRENTS 31, no. 4 (April 2005): 42–47.
www.case.org/Publications_and_Products/CURRENTS/CURRENTS_Archive/2005/April_2005/A_Picture_of_Health.html.

———. "A Quantitative Model for Evaluating Advancement Effectiveness." *CASE International Journal of Educational Advancement* 4, no. 2 (October 2003): 166–78.
www.palgrave-journals.com/ijea/journal/v4/n2/pdf/2140022a.pdf.

Walker, Theresa. "Why So Formal? Both Young and Old Appreciate a Little Online Respect." CURRENTS 30, no. 4 (April 2004): 6.
www.case.org/Publications_and_Products/CURRENTS/CURRENTS_Archive/2004/April_2004/AdvanceWork_Why_So_Formal.html.

CASE STUDIES

Carleton University. "A Ringing Endorsement." 2005 CASE Circle of Excellence Silver Award in Alumni Relations Programs—Alumni Programs.
www.case.org/Documents/protected/Awards/Circle_of_Excellence/2005_COE_Winners/1_Alumni_Relations/1b_Carleton.pdf.

During a period of fiscal restraint in 2001–02, Carleton University's Office of Advancement stopped mailing the university magazine to its 1,800 international alumni. The result was devastating. Alumni complained that they felt disconnected, and the university lost contact with many of them. In February 2004, Carleton launched a successful online contest, "A Ringing Endorsement," that helped international alumni reconnect with alma mater, inspired goodwill and alumni pride and helped the university collect updated contact information from many overseas graduates.

Imperial College London. "International Ambassadors Scheme." 2008 CASE Circle of Excellence Silver Award in Alumni Relations Programs—Programming for Special Constituencies.
www.case.org/award_programs/circle_of_excellence/2008_winners/1c_imperial_college_london_2008_silver_award_abstract.html.

The Imperial College International Ambassador Scheme was launched in September 2006 to enhance the way the college engages alumni who live outside the U.K. The scheme gives international alumni exposure to senior members of the college administration and faculty, enhances services for overseas alumni, provides college updates from those who experience and influence college life, enables established international alumni groups to use ambassador events to gain new active members, helps inactive groups to revive activities and enables senior staff members to actively contribute to relationship building with alumni.

NAFSA: Association of International Educators, a professional association located in the United States, has collected several case studies of international alumni relations programs. All case studies are linked from
www.nafsa.org/knowledge_community_network.sec/international_student_3/ international_student_4/practice_resources_18/advising_and_training/ international_alumni/.

- Ball State University Office of International Advancement
- Michigan State University International Alumni Academic Internship Program
- Texas A&M University Latin American Network
- Texas Tech University International Alumni Relations Program
- University of Arkansas International Alumni Reunion
- University of Miami Intensive English Program Alumni Network
- University of Oregon International Alumni Program

Tufts University. "Tufts World Day." 2007 CASE Circle of Excellence Gold Award in Alumni Relations—Alumni Programs.
www.case.org/Award_Programs/Circle_of_Excellence/2007_Winners/1b_Tufts_ University_2007_Gold_Medal_Abstract.html.

On Oct. 19, 2006, Tufts University Alumni Association invited all regional chapters to participate in Tufts World Day, a series of orchestrated events around the world that celebrated the university's networks of alumni, parents, students and friends. Tufts World Day promoted a connectedness among alumni and back to alma mater just two weeks before the public launch of "Beyond Boundaries: The Campaign for Tufts."

SATELLITE OFFICES

Frankle, Rivi. "Advancement Away from Home: The Challenges and Rewards of Setting Up Shop Halfway Around the World." CURRENTS 25, no. 9 (October 1999): 11–12.
www.case.org/Publications_and_Products/CURRENTS/CURRENTS_Archive/1999/ October_1999/Managers_Portfolio_Advancement_Away_from_Home.html.

Kirkwood, Donald. "Satellite Offices in International Fundraising." In *Across Frontiers: New International Perspectives on Educational Fundraising,* ed. John Mc Loughlin and Jane Joo Park, 73–85. Washington, DC: CASE, 2010.

Koenig, Bonnie L. *Going Global for the Greater Good: Succeeding as a Nonprofit in the International Community.* San Francisco: Jossey-Bass, 2004.

Santiago, Kim. "Foreign Affairs: The University of Wisconsin Establishes an Advancement Office in Japan." CURRENTS 35, no. 9 (November/December 2009): 13–14. *www.case.org/Publications_and_Products/CURRENTS/CURRENTS_Archive/2009/ NovemberDecember_2009/Office_Space_Foreign_Affairs.html.*

Walker, Theresa. "Going The Distance: What Your Institution Should Know about Satellite Offices." CURRENTS 28, no. 8 (October 2001): 10. *www.case.org/Publications_and_Products/CURRENTS/CURRENTS_Archive/2001/ October_2001/AdvanceWork_Going_the_Distance.html.*

Worth, Steven M. *The Association Guide to Going Global: New Strategies for a Changing Economic Landscape.* Hoboken, NJ: Wiley, 2010.

SOCIAL MEDIA

Fernandez, Kim. "Following the Threads: Connections, Conversations, and Community in the New Social Media Space," CURRENTS 36, no. 7 (September 2010): 16–23. *www.case.org/Publications_and_Products/CURRENTS/CURRENTS_Archive/2010/ September_2010/Following__the_Threads.html.*

Isurus Market Research and Consulting. "Use of Technology for Development and Alumni Relations among CASE Members." Report prepared for CASE and SunGard Higher Education. July 2010. *www.case.org/Documents/protected/whitepapers/ UseOfTechnologyForDevelopmentAndAlumniRelations2010.pdf.*

Lavrusik, Vadim. "10 Ways Universities Are Engaging Alumni Using Social Media." *Mashable*, 2009. *mashable.com/2009/07/23/alumni-social-media/.*

LeCouvie, Leisha. "The Use of Social Media for Alumni Relations and University Development." Presented at the Council of Alumni Association Executives Summer Institute, Montreal, July 2009. *www.mstonerblog.com/images/uploads/LeCouvie_Rpt.pdf.*

Makrez, Heather M. "Am I Invited? Social Media and Alumni Relations." In *Higher Education Administration with Social Media: Including Applications in Student Affairs, Enrollment Management, Alumni Relations, and Career Centers,* 229–48. Bingley, UK: Emerald Group, 2011.

Moore, Robert M. "The Sea of Social Media: Navigating the Digital World Using Your Strategic Plan." CURRENTS 35, no. 9 (November/December 2009): 30–35.
www.case.org/Publications_and_Products/CURRENTS/CURRENTS_Archive/2009/NovemberDecember_2009/The_Sea_of_Social_Media.html.

Nekritz, Tim. "Location, Location, Location: Where Do Location-based Services Fit into Your Institution's Social Media Mix?" CURRENTS 37, no. 1 (January 2011): 32–35.
www.case.org/Publications_and_Products/CURRENTS/CURRENTS_Archive/2011/January_2011/Location_Location_Location.html.

Pearson, Jerold. "Sizing Up Social Media: New Research Shows That Peer-to-Peer Interaction Provides Value to the Institution." CURRENTS 36, no. 7 (September 2010): 24–27.
www.case.org/Publications_and_Products/CURRENTS/CURRENTS_Archive/2010/September_2010/Sizing_Up_Social_Media.html.

Pulley, John. "In Full Bloom: Technology Takes Root in Advancement." CURRENTS 36, no. 2 (February 2010): 16–21.
www.case.org/Publications_and_Products/CURRENTS/CURRENTS_Archive/2010/February_2010/In_Full_Bloom.html.

Reuben, Rachel L. "Strategic View: Managing Social Media Is a Team Sport." CURRENTS 37, no. 1 (January 2011): 13–14.
www.case.org/Publications_and_Products/CURRENTS/CURRENTS_Archive/2011/January_2011/Office_Space_Strategic_View.html.

Scully, Maura King. "Into the Mainstream: Alumni Offices Need to Stop Analyzing Online Social Networking and Just Do It." CURRENTS 35, no. 1 (January 2009): 16–21.
www.case.org/Publications_and_Products/CURRENTS/CURRENTS_Archive/2009/January_2009/Into_the_Mainstream.html.

Shaindlin, Andrew, and Elizabeth Allen. "Alumni Networks and Twitter: An Update." Alumni Futures White Paper no. 3, 2010.
alumnifutures.typepad.com/files/af-alumni-twitter-update-2_10.pdf.

Slover-Linett, Cheryl, and Michael Stoner. "Social Experiments: Results from CASE's Inaugural Survey of Social Media in Advancement." CURRENTS 36, no. 9 (November/December 2010): 32–39.
www.case.org/Publications_and_Products/CURRENTS/CURRENTS_Archive/2010/NovemberDecember_2010/Social_Experiments.html.

———. "Succeeding with Social Media: Lessons from the First Survey of Social Media in Advancement." CASE white paper. 2010.
www.case.org/Documents/protected/whitepapers/mStoner-SloverLinett_SM.pdf.

Steggles, Andy. *Social Networking for Nonprofits: Increasing Engagement in a Mobile and Web 2.0 World*. Washington, DC: ASAE and the Center for Association Leadership, 2010.

Ward, Brad J. "Bird on a Wire: Is Twitter the Next Big Thing or Dead on Arrival?" CURRENTS 36, no. 5 (May/June 2010): 32–36. *www.case.org/Publications_and_Products/CURRENTS/CURRENTS_Archive/2010/ MayJune_2010/Bird_on_a_Wire.html*.

STRATEGIC PLANNING

Bryson, John M. *Strategic Planning for Public and Nonprofit Organizations: A Guide to Strengthening and Sustaining Organizational Achievement*, 3rd ed. San Francisco: Jossey-Bass, 2004.

Bryson, John M., and Farnum K. Alston. *Creating and Implementing Your Strategic Plan: A Workbook for Public and Nonprofit Organizations*, 2nd ed. San Francisco: Jossey-Bass, 2005.

Davies, Robert O. "Love Thy Enemy: Embrace Strategic Planning and Make It Work for You." CURRENTS 31, no. 8 (September 2005): 11–12. *www.case.org/Publications_and_Products/CURRENTS/CURRENTS_Archive/2005/ September_2005/Managers_Portfolio_Love_Thy_Enemy.html*.

Dooris, M. J. "Two Decades of Strategic Planning." *Planning for Higher Education* 31, no. 2 (Summer 2003): 32–36. *www.psu.edu/president/cqi/planning_research/reports/twodecades.pdf*.

Hadley, Jacquelyn, Laura Lanzerotti, and Adam Nathan. *Living Into Your Strategic Plan: A Guide to Implementation That Gets Results*. Bridgespan Group, 2011. *www.bridgespan.org/living-into-your-strategic-plan.aspx*.

Haviland, David. "Broad Strokes, Fine Brush: Translating the Institutional Plan into an Advancement Plan." CURRENTS 31, no. 2 (February 2005): 36–39. *www.case.org/Publications_and_Products/CURRENTS/CURRENTS_Archive/2005/ February_2005/Broad_Strokes_Fine_Brush.html*.

Noel-Bentley, Pommashea. "Leveraging the Balanced Scorecard to Measure Accountability in Alumni Relations." Master's thesis, Athabasca University, 2003.

Scully, Maura King. "Seamless Integration: Alumni Associations Move to Align Programming with Their Institution's Strategic Plan." CURRENTS 36, no. 8 (October 2010): 30–35. *www.case.org/Publications_and_Products/CURRENTS/CURRENTS_Archive/2010/ October_2010/Seamless_Integration.html*.

Sevier, Robert A. "From Strategy to Action: Your Goal Is Not the Creation of a Strategic Plan, but of a Guide to Action." *University Business* (March 2003). *findarticles.com/p/articles/mi_m0LSH/is_2_6/ai_102554426/*.

———. *Strategic Planning in Higher Education: Theory and Practice.* Washington, DC: CASE, 2000.

Stenko, Michael. "'Are We There Yet?': Strategic Planning in Alumni Relations." In *Alumni Relations: A Newcomer's Guide to Success*, 2nd ed., ed. John A. Feudo, 81–93. Washington, DC: CASE, 2010.

Note: The acronym IAR is used in this index in place of the phrase *international alumni relations.*

ABOUT THE AUTHOR

With over two decades of experience in higher education and constituent relations, Dr. Gretchen Dobson is a leading global alumni relations consultant developing international advancement programs for educational institutions and non-profit organizations around the world. Gretchen Dobson LLC builds volunteer networks to advance internationalization goals such as student recruitment, academic programs, international philanthropy and overall reputational management and branding.

Dobson was recognized by the *Chronicle of Higher Education* as one of the leading "Innovators in Internationalization" for her work at Tufts University. She is a member of the Board of Directors for United Planet, a global network of leaders and volunteers fostering cross-cultural understanding and addressing shared challenges to unite the world in a community beyond borders.

Dobson received her B.A. and M.A. from Boston College, and her Ed.D. in higher education management from the University of Pennsylvania. She currently lives in Chengdu, China.

ABOUT CASE

The Council for Advancement and Support of Education (CASE) is the professional organization for advancement professionals at all levels who work in alumni relations, communications and marketing, development and advancement services.

CASE's membership includes more than 3,600 colleges, universities and independent and secondary schools in nearly 80 countries. This makes CASE one of the largest nonprofit education associations in the world in terms of institutional membership. CASE also serves more than 78,000 advancement professionals on staffs of member institutions and has more than 18,000 individual members and more than 220 Educational Partner corporate members.

CASE has offices in Washington, D.C., London, Singapore and Mexico City. The association produces high-quality and timely content, publications, conferences, institutes and workshops that assist advancement professionals perform more effectively and serve their institutions.

For more information, visit *www.case.org* or call +1-202-328-2273.